THE
'X' CHRONICLES NEWSPAPER
Fact Is Fiction and Fiction Is Reality Since 1992

Vol. 23, No 8

A REL-MAR McConnell Media Company Publication

AUGUST 2014 $4.95 US

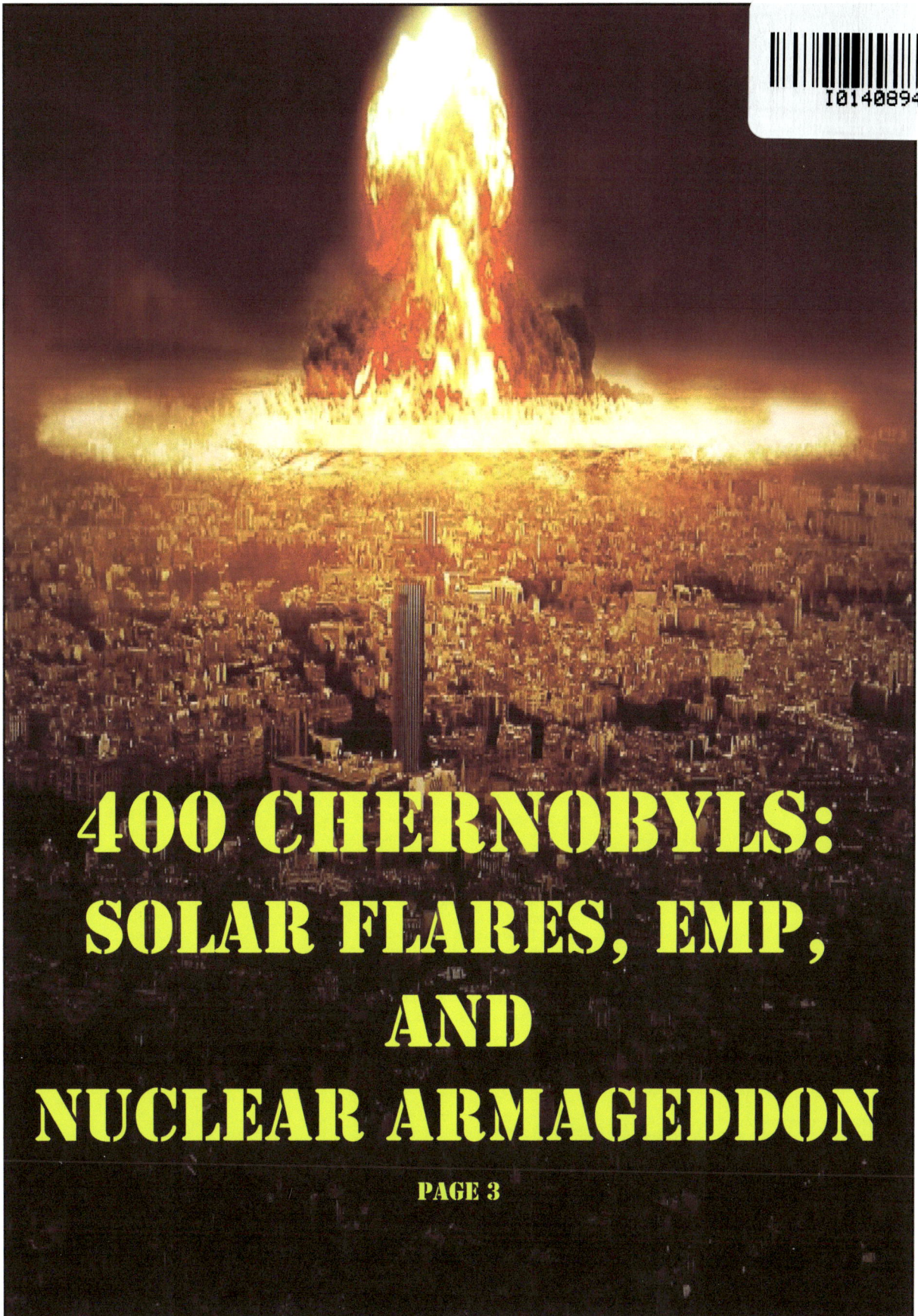

400 CHERNOBYLS: SOLAR FLARES, EMP, AND NUCLEAR ARMAGEDDON

PAGE 3

In This Edition of The 'X' Chronicles Newspaper

AUGUST 2014 - 72 Pages

These are just **SOME** of the stories and articles in this edition of
THE 'X' CHRONICLES NEWSPAPER

Page 02: The REL-MAR Multimedia App
Page 03: Matt Stein : 400 Chernobyls: Solar Flares, EMP, and Nuclear Armageddon
Page 07: When Disaster Strikes (A)
Page 11: UFOs Through The Ages
Page 13: Hidden History
Page 14: Dan Perkins : OPED - An Army Is Invading American!
Page 15: Rob McConnell : St Catharines Poltergeist of 1970
Page 16: You Can Beat Lung Cancer (A)
Page 18: The 'X' Zone Directory of Who's Who
Page 20: The Flying Dutchman & Other Phantom Ships
Page 22: Prism Publishing (A)
Page 23: Africa's Unfinished Symphony (A)
Page 26: The Power of the Mayan (A)
Page 27: Till The End Of Time (A)
Page 28: Lost Powers
Page 29: Secrets Of My Soul (A)
Page 31: Looking Into Death
Page 33: Angels! (A)
Page 34: Time Will Tell (A)
Page 36: Who Is This Babylon? (A)
Page 38: The Very First UFOs Were Terrestrial
Page 39: Howard Bloom : Instant Evolution
Page 41: Theatre of the Mind (A)
Page 43: Living Whole, Living Well (A)
Page 44: From Out of the Woodwork (A)
Page 46: You Can Make A Real Change In 2014 (A)
Page 47: CCC Publishing (A)
Page 49: Asian Health Secrets (A)
Page 50: Razor Of Madness (A)
Page 54: Kooch Daniels Cybermystic (A)
Page 57: The Mohammad Code (A)
Page 58: Use Of Body Cams By Law Enforcement
Page 59: A Guiding Lite (A)
Page 60: The Psychology Of Alien Abduction
Page 61: J Allan Danelek : Understanding The Psychology Of Ghosts
Page 64: Metaphysician Tara Tarot (A)
Page 66: Liquid Diamond (A)
Page 67: Conspiracy Theories
Page 68: In Memory of Robin Williams
Page 70: Bobcha's Corner
Page 71: Prevagen (A)
Page 72: Future of God Amen (A)

The 'X' Chronicles Newspaper is published by REL-MAR McConnell Media Company. The contents of this material are (C) Copyright 1992-2014 by REL-MAR McConnell Media Company and may not be copied or reprinted in whole or in part without the express written consent of the publisher. All opinions, comments or statements of fact expressed by Rob McConnell's guests are strictly their own and are not to be construed as those of or in any manner endorsed by REL-MAR McConnell Media Company, Rob McConnell, The 'X' Chronicles Newspaper, The 'X' Zone Radio & TV Show, its affiliated stations or employees or advertisers. REL-MAR McConnell Media Company assumes no responsibility for claims made by its advertisers, contributors or stories from other sources and do not endorse any product and or service mentioned herein. To advertise in The 'X' Chronicles, please contact us at Toll Free at (800) 610-7035 or send an email to: publisher@xchronicles-newspaper.com

The REL-MAR MULTIMEDIA APP Is Here For Only $0.99!

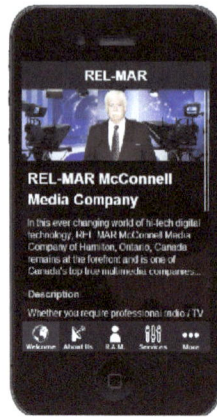

Available for Android, Apple, Kindle Fire

Whether you are a believer or a skeptic when it comes to the world of the paranormal or science of parapsychology, you will enjoy listening to The 'X' Zone Radio Show with Rob McConnell which has been broadcasting since 1992 on terrestrial radio stations and internet audio feeds and networks... reading The 'X' Chronicles Newspaper, the world's only Paranormal / Parapsychology newspaper which has been published monthly since January 1992... watching videos from 'X' Zone TV and much more.

Since hitting the broadcast airwaves, Rob McConnell has interviewed more than 3,800 guests including scientists, experiencers, witnesses, believers, skeptics, actors, authors, religious leaders, government officials and those who claim to have the ability to communicate with those on the other side.

Topics that are discussed and investigated on The 'X' Zone Radio/TV Show and read in The 'X' Chronicles Newspaper include, but are not limited to: 11:11, 666: The Number Of The Beast, Alien Abduction, Aliens, Angels, Apocalypse, Astrology, Atlantis, Bible, Chinese Astrology, Conspiracy Theories, Cosmology, Crop Circles, Cryptozoology, Crystals, Demonology, Dreams And Dream Interpretation, Electronic Voice Phenomena, End Times, End-Time Prophecies, ESP, Exorcism, Extraterrestrial Communication, Fairies, Forbidden Knowledge, Ghosts, Government Cover-ups, Hauntings, Herbalism, Kennedy Assassination, Kirlian Photography, Life After Death, Lost Tribes And Civilizations, Mind Over Matter, Near-Death Experience, Nostradamus, Numerology, Occult, Ouija Boards, Palmistry, Paranormal Hoaxes And Frauds, Paranormal, Parapsychology, Past Life Regression, Precognition, PSI, Psychic Phenomena, Psychic Phenomenon, Psychic Surgery, Raelians, Reincarnation, Remote Viewing, Sacred Geometry, Science Fiction, Séances, Shadow People, Shamanism, Spiritualists, Tarot Cards, The Apocalypse, The Bermuda Triangle, The Dalai Lama, The Dead Sea Scrolls, The Michigan Triangle, Time Travel, UFO Crashes, UFOs, Unsolved Mysteries, Vile Vortices, VooDoo, Wicca, Zombies. You will be able to browse the 'X' Zone broadcast schedule and in our "Coupon" section, you will be able to enjoy money saving specials - only available to users of the REL-MAR Multimedia App.

www.thexzonestore.com

The 'X' Zone Radio & TV Show with Rob McConnell

The 'X' Zone Radio & TV Show is heard Monday - Friday from 10 PM to 2 AM Eastern, and then the show is repeated in its entirety from 2 AM - 6 AM on the 'X' ZONE BROADCAST NETWORK family broadcast of affiliates throughout world on TelStar 12 America, TelStar 12 Europe, Galaxy XI, IntelSat 801, NSS-K, PAS-1R, Atlantic Bird 2, II-F4,and Agilia 2.We also deliver The 'X' Zone Radio and TV Show to broadcasters and satellite programmers via a secure and encrypted FTP server.

Some 'X' Zone Affiliates Past & Present

KKRP AM 1610 - Oklahoma
AM 1590 WPUL - Daytona Beach FL
AM 1150 KHRO - El Paso TX
AM 1600 KOHI - St. Helens OR
AM 1350 KCHR - Charleston MO
AM 1400 WZNG - Shelbyville / Nashville TN
TalkStar 840 - Titusville, Orlando, Mims FL
FM 107.7 WMEX - Rochester NH
FM 89.7 KNTS - John Day OR
AM 1330 WELW - Cleveland OH
AM 1340 KSEK - Pittsburgh KS
AM 1510 WDRF - Woodruff SC
AM 1600 KOHI - St Helens OR
FM 104.7 KEIF, Enid, OK
AM 1320 WARL - New Bedofrd, MA
FM 99.1 KRUP - Dillingham, AK
AM 1150 KHRO - El Paso, TX
AM 1590 WPUL - Daytona Beach, FL
X Files Paranormal Network
America Talk Radio
UKHDRadio
EURO-HDRadio
AM 630 CKOV - Kelowna BC
AM 580 CFRA - Ottawa ON
AM 920 CJCH - Halifax NS
AM 1330 CHLW - St. Paul, AB
FM 104 CJSB - Swan Lake, MB
FM 90.1 CHMZ - Tofino, BC
FM 99.5 CIMM - Ucluelet, BC
FM 98.9 CFPV - Pemberton, BC
AM 1620 WDHP - Frederikstead USVI
UK High Definition Radio
Turquoise Radio
27 Asian Countries, Including...
The Philippines
China
Hong Kong
Taiwan
Korea
Africa
India
Europe
STAR CABLE - Asia

The 'X' Zone Radio Show and The 'X' Zone TV Show is now available at Apple iTunes!
Our past shows are available at
http://xzone.rnn.libsynpro.com/rss

The 'X' Zone TV Show
KHPK CH 28 - Dallas/Fort Worth, Texas
WBQP CH 12 (Cable 75) - Pensacola, Florida
WBCF CH 3 - Florence/Muscle Shoals, Alabama
WXLF CH 5 - Florence/Muscle Shoals, Alabama
KWVT CH 52 (Cable 7) - Salem, Oregon
WDRL CH 24 (digital 41) - Roanoke/Lynchburg, Virginia
KCTU CH 41 - Wichita, Kansas
KBGN CH 59 - Pittsburgh, Pennsylvania
Western Cable Service - Sequim, Washington
KLFA TV Channel 8, Los Angeles, California.
Cable in Guatemala and parts of Central America
NNTV Niagara Now TV - Ontario, Canada

400 Chernobyls:
Solar Flares, EMP, andNuclear Armageddon

400 Chernobyls:
Solar Flares, EMP, and Nuclear Armageddon

By Matthew Stein, P.E

There are nearly 450 nuclear reactors in the world, with hundreds more either under construction or in the planning stages. There are 104 of these reactors in the USA and 195 in Europe. Imagine what havoc it would wreak on our civilization and the planet's ecosystems if we were to suddenly witness not just one or two nuclear melt-downs but 400 or more! How likely is it that our world might experience an event that could ultimately cause hundreds of reactors to fail and melt down at approximately the same time? I venture to say that, unless we take significant protective measures, this apocalyptic scenario is not only possible but probable.

Consider the ongoing problems caused by three reactor core meltdowns, explosions, and breached containment vessels at Japan's Fukushima Daiichi facility, and the subsequent health and environmental issues. Consider the millions of innocent victims that have already

died or continue to suffer from horrific radiation-related health problems ("Chernobyl AIDS", epidemic cancers, chronic fatigue, etc) resulting from the Chernobyl reactor explosions, fires, and fallout. If just two serious nuclear disasters, spaced 25 years apart, could cause such horrendous environmental catastrophes, it is hard to imagine how we could ever hope to recover from hundreds of similar nuclear incidents occurring simultaneously across the planet. Since more than one third of all Americans live within 50 miles of a nuclear power plant, this is a serious issue that should be given top priority![1]

In the past 152 years, Earth has been struck roughly 100 solar storms causing significant geomagnetic disturbances (GMD), two of which were powerful enough to rank as "extreme GMDs". If an extreme GMD of such magnitude were to occur today, in all likelihood it would initiate a chain of events leading to catastrophic failures at the vast majority of our world's nuclear reactors, quite similar to the disasters at both Chernobyl and Fukushima, but multiplied over 100 times. When massive solar flares launch a huge mass of highly charged plasma (a coronal mass ejection, or CME) directly towards Earth, colliding with our planet's outer atmosphere and magnetosphere, the result is a significant geomagnetic disturbance.

Since an extreme GMD of such a potentially disruptive magnitude that it would collapse the grid across most of the US last

Coronal Mass Ejection (CME), SOHO image, June 9, 2002.

occurred in May of 1921, long before the advent of modern electronics, widespread electric power grids, and nuclear power plants, we are for the most part blissfully unaware of this threat and totally unprepared for its consequences. The good news is that there are some relatively affordable protective equipment and processes which could be installed to protect critical components in the electric power grid and its nuclear reactors, thereby protecting our civilization from this "end-of-the-world-as-we-know-it" scenario. The bad news is that, as of now, even though panels of scientists and engineers have studied the problem, and the bi-partisan congressional EMP commission has presented a list of specific recommendations to congress, our leaders have yet to approve and implement a single significant preventative measure!

Most of us believe something like this could never happen, and if it could, certainly our "authorities" would do everything in their power to make sure they would prevent such an Apocalypse from ever taking place. Unfortunately, the opposite is true. "How could this happen?" you might ask. "Is this truly possible?" Read and weep, for you will soon know the answer.

Continued On Page 4

400 Chernobyls:
Solar Flares, EMP, and Nuclear Armageddon
Continued From Page 3

Nuclear Power Plants and the Electric Power Grid

Our global system of electrical power generation and distribution ("the grid"), upon which every facet of our modern life is utterly dependent, in its current form is extremely vulnerable to severe geomagnetic storms of a magnitude that tends to strike our planet on an average of approximately once every 70 to 100 years. We depend on this grid to maintain food production and distribution, telecommunications, Internet services, medical services, military defense, transportation, government, water treatment, sewage and garbage removal, refrigeration, oil refining and gas pumping, and to conduct all forms of commerce.

Unfortunately, the world's nuclear power plants, as they are currently designed, are critically dependent upon maintaining connection to a functioning electrical grid, for all but relatively short periods of electrical blackouts, in order to keep their reactor cores continuously cooled so as to avoid catastrophic reactor core meltdowns and spent fuel rod storage pond fires.

If an extreme GMD were to cause widespread grid collapse (which it most certainly will), in as little as one or two hours after each nuclear reactor facility's backup generators either fail to start, or run out of fuel, the reactor cores will start to melt down. After a few days without electricity to run the cooling system pumps, the water bath covering the spent fuel rods stored in "spent fuel ponds" will boil away, allowing the stored fuel rods to melt down and burn [2]. Since the Nuclear Regulatory Commission (NRC) currently mandates that only one week's supply of backup generator fuel needs to be stored at each reactor site, it is likely that after we witness the spectacular night-time celestial light show from the next extreme GMD we will have about one week in which to prepare ourselves for Armageddon.

To do nothing is to behave like ostriches with our heads in the sand, blindly believing that "everything will be okay," as our world inexorably drifts towards the next naturally recurring, 100% inevitable, super solar storm and resultant extreme GMD. The result of which in short order will end the industrialized world as we know it, incurring almost incalculable suffering, death, and environmental destruction on a scale not seen since the extinction of the dinosaurs some 65 million years ago.

The End of "The Grid" As We Know It

There are records from the 1850s to today of roughly one hundred significant geomagnetic solar storms, two of which in the last 25 years were strong enough to cause millions of dollars worth of damage to key components that keep our modern grid powered. In March of 1989, a severe solar storm induced powerful electric currents in grid wiring that fried a main power transformer in the HydroQuebec system, causing a cascading grid failure that knocked out power to 6 million customers for nine hours while also damaging similar transformers in New Jersey and the United Kingdom. More recently, in 2003 a solar storm of lesser intensity, but longer duration, caused a blackout in Sweden and induced powerful currents in the South African grid that severely damaged or destroyed fourteen of their major power transformers, impairing commerce and comfort over major portions of that country as they were forced to resort to massive rolling blackouts that dragged on for many months[3].

During the Great Geomagnetic Storm of May 14-15, 1921, brilliant aurora displays were reported in the Northern Hemisphere as far south as Mexico and Puerto Rico, and in the Southern Hemisphere as far north as Samoa[5]. This extreme GMD produced ground currents roughly ten times as strong as the 1989 Quebec incident. Just 62 years earlier, the great granddaddy of recorded GMDs, referred to as "The Carrington Event," raged from August 28 to September 4, 1859. This extreme GMD induced currents so powerful that telegraph lines, towers, and stations caught on fire at a number of locations around the world. Best estimates are that the Carrington Event was approximately 50% stronger than the Great Geomagnetic Storm of 1921[6]. Since we are headed into an active solar period, much like the one preceding the Carrington Event, scientists are concerned that conditions could be ripe for the next extreme GMD[7].

Prior to the advent of the microchip and modern extra-high-voltage (EHV) transformers (key grid components that were first introduced in the late 1960's), most electrical systems were relatively robust and resistant to the effects of GMDs. Given the fact that a simple electrostatic spark can fry a microchip, and many thousands of miles of power lines act like giant antennas for capturing massive amounts of GMD spawned electromagnetic energy, the electrical systems of the modern world are far more vulnerable than their predecessors.

A growing number of scientists and engineers have become concerned about the vulnerability of both the grid and modern microelectronics to debilitating damage from severe electromagnetic disturbances. These could come either in the form of naturally occurring extreme GMDs, like what occurred during the 1921 and 1859 super solar storms, or an electromagnetic pulse (EMP) resulting from the deliberate detonation of a nuclear device at a high altitude above the earth.

The federal government recently sponsored a detailed scientific study to more fully understand the extent to which critical components of our national electrical power grid might be effected by either a naturally occurring GMD or a man-made EMP. Under the auspices of the EMP Commission and the Federal Emergency Management Agency (FEMA), and reviewed in depth by the Oakridge National Laboratory and the National Academy of Sciences, Metatech corporation undertook extensive modeling and analysis of the potential effects of extreme geomagnetic storms upon the U.S. electrical power grid. They based their modeling upon a storm of intensity equal to the Great Geomagnetic Storm of 1921. Metatech estimated that within the continental United States alone, these voltage and current spikes combined with harmonic anomalies would severely damage or destroy over 350 EHV power transformers critical to the functioning of the U.S. grid, and possibly well over 2000 EHV transformers worldwide.[8]

EHV transformers are custom designed for each installation and are made to order, weighing as much as 300 tons each, and costing well over US 1$ million each. Given the fact that there is currently a three year waiting list for a single EHV transformer (due to recent demand from China and India, the lead times have grown from one to three years), and that the total global manufacturing capacity is roughly 100 EHV transformers per year when the world's manufacturing centers are functioning properly, you can begin to grasp the dire implications of this situation.

Continued on Page 5

400 Chernobyls:
Solar Flares, EMP, and Nuclear Armageddon
Continued From Page 4

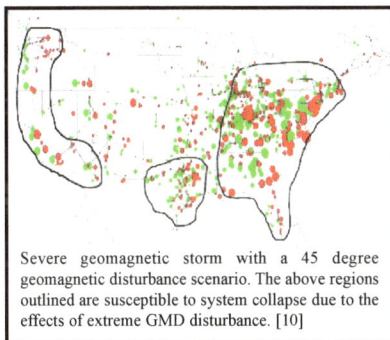

Growth of the US High Voltage Transmission Network and the Annual Electric Energy Usage over the Past 50 Years. In addition to increasing total network size, the network has grown in complexity with the introduction of higher-kilovolt rated lines that subsequently also tend to carry larger GIC (geomagnetically induced current) flows. (Grid size derived from data in the EHV Transmission Line Reference Book and the NERC Electricity Supply and Demand database; energy usage statistics from the US Department of Energy – Energy Information Administration.) [9]

The loss of thousands of EHV transformers worldwide would cause a catastrophic collapse of the grid, stretching across much of the industrialized world. It will take years at best for the industrialized world to put itself back together after such an event, especially considering the fact that most of the manufacturing centers that make this equipment will also be grappling with widespread grid failure.

Since the earth's magnetic field tends to protect the tropical latitudes from the most damaging geomagnetic effects, with protection dropping as one travels closer to the poles, perhaps the infrastructure and manufacturing zones in places like Mexico, Malaysia, India, and Singapore will be spared. However, most of those countries probably also rely on goods and services imported from other parts of the world that would be crippled for many months (or years) in the event of a an extreme GMD.

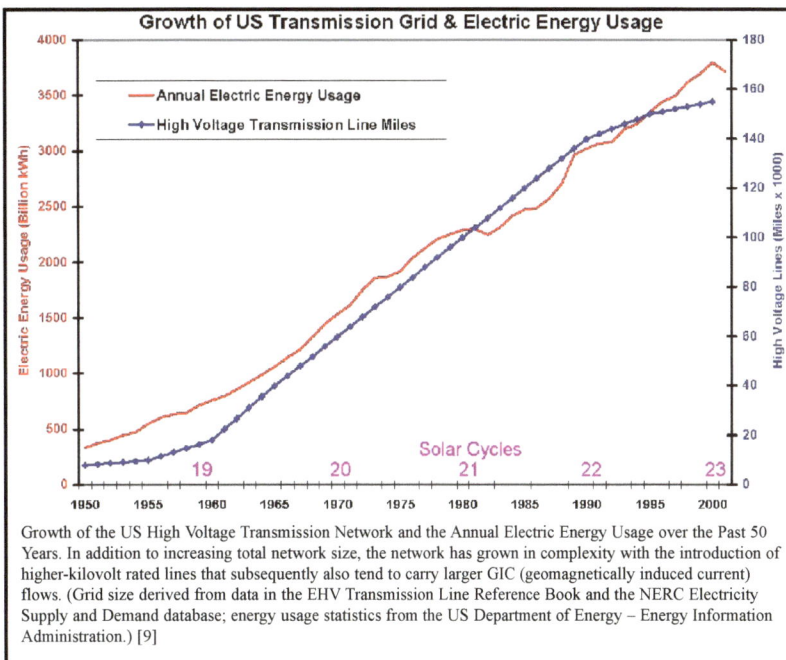

Severe geomagnetic storm with a 45 degree geomagnetic disturbance scenario. The above regions outlined are susceptible to system collapse due to the effects of extreme GMD disturbance. [10]

According to the various Metatech analyses, it is estimated that grid collapse will effect at least 130 million people in the United States alone. However, in a recent personal conversation, John Kappenman (author of the Metatech study) admitted that this estimate is probably grossly optimistic.[11] He noted that "killer trees" and other seemingly insignificant events have been attributed to being the tiny seeds that sprouted into giant multi-state blackouts. The massive Western States Blackout of August 10, 1996, apparently started when sagging power lines shorted against improperly pruned trees in Oregon during a triple-digit heat wave, cascading into a blackout that cut power to seven western states, parts of Baja, Mexico, and two Canadian provinces. Due to excessive loads from millions of air-conditioning units operating during the heat wave, the grid had been operating near peak capacity and the shorted lines threw it over the edge into cascading failure, affecting millions of customers[12].

A similar group of "killer trees" in the state of Ohio were apparently the root cause of the Great Northeastern Blackout of August 2003 that cut power to over 50 million people [13]. Kappenman also cited the recent September 2011 event where a utility technician flipped a switch to bypass a large series capacitor that was not working properly at a substation outside

of Yuma Arizona, and for reasons not fully understood this caused a chain of events leading to a massive cascading blackout that cut power to millions of customers in Arizona, California, and Mexico. This same blackout also caused two nuclear reactors at the San Onofre nuclear power plant to automatically shut down and go off line, which they are designed to do as a safety precaution in the event of a local grid failure. This exacerbated the situation by reducing the locally available generating capacity at the same time as utility workers were desperately trying to restore power to San Diego and other areas[14].

Our Nuclear "Achilles Heel"

Five years ago I visited the still highly contaminated areas of Ukraine and the Belarus border where much of the radioactive plume from Chernobyl descended on 26 April 1986. I challenge chief scientist John Beddington and environmentalists like George Monbiot or any of the pundits now downplaying the risks of radiation to talk to the doctors, the scientists, the mothers, children and villagers who have been left with the consequences of a major nuclear accident. It was grim. We went from hospital to hospital and from one contaminated village to another. We found deformed and genetically mutated babies in the wards; pitifully sick children in the homes; adolescents with stunted growth and dwarf torsos; fetuses without thighs or fingers and villagers who told us every member of their family was sick. This was 20 years after the accident, but we heard of many unusual clusters of people with rare bone cancers.... Villages testified that 'the Chernobyl necklace'—thyroid cancer—was so common as to be unremarkable.

— **John Vidal, "Nuclear's Green Cheerleaders Forget Chernobyl at Our Peril," Guardian. co.uk, April 1, 2011[15]**

So what do extended grid blackouts have to do with potential nuclear catastrophes? Nuclear power plants are designed to disconnect automatically from the grid in the event of a local power failure or major grid anomaly, and once disconnected they begin the process of shutting down the reactor's core. In the event of the loss of coolant flow to an active nuclear reactor's core, the reactor will start to melt down and fail catastrophically within a matter of a few hours at most. In an extreme GMD, nearly every reactor in the world could be affected.

It was a short-term cooling system failure that caused the partial reactor core meltdown in March 1979 at Three Mile Island, Pennsylvania. Similarly, according to Japanese authorities it was not direct damage from Japan's 9.0 magnitude Tohoku Earthquake on March 11, 2011 that caused the Fukushima Daiichi nuclear reactor disaster, but the loss of electric power to the reactor's cooling system pumps when the reactor's backup batteries and diesel generators were wiped out by the ensuing tidal waves. In the hours and days after the tidal waves shuttered the cooling systems, the cores of reactors number 1, 2, and 3 were in full meltdown and released hydrogen gas, fueling explosions which breached several reactor containment vessels and blew the roof off the building housing the spent fuel storage pond of reactor number 4.

Of even greater danger and concern than the reactor cores themselves are the spent fuel rods stored in on-site cooling ponds. Lacking a permanent spent nuclear fuel storage facility, so-called "temporary" nuclear fuel containment ponds are features common to nearly all nuclear reactor facilities. They typically contain the accumulated spent fuel from 10 or more decommissioned reactor cores. Due to lack of a permanent repository, most of these fuel containment ponds are greatly overloaded and tightly packed beyond original design. They are generally surrounded by common light industrial buildings, with concrete walls and corrugated steel roofs. *(Continued on Page 5)*

400 Chernobyls:
Solar Flares, EMP, and Nuclear Armageddon
Continued From Page 5

Unlike the active reactor cores, which are encased inside massive "containment vessels" with thick walls of concrete and steel, the buildings surrounding spent fuel rod storage ponds would do practically nothing to contain radioactive contaminants in the event of prolonged cooling system failures.

Since spent fuel ponds typically hold far greater quantities of highly radioactive material then the active nuclear reactors locked inside reinforced containment vessels, they clearly present far greater potential for the catastrophic spread of highly radioactive contaminants over huge swaths of land, polluting the environment for multiple generations spanning hundreds of years. A study by the Nuclear Regulatory Commission (NRC) determined that the "boil down time" for spent fuel rod containment ponds runs from between 4 and 22 days after loss of cooling system power before degenerating into a Fukushima-like situation, depending upon the type of nuclear reactor and how recently its latest batch of fuel rods had been decommissioned[16].

Reactor fuel rods have a protective zirconium cladding, which if superheated while exposed to air will burn with intense self-generating heat, much like a magnesium fire, releasing highly radioactive aerosols and smoke. According to Arnie Gundersen, former Senior Vice President for Nuclear Engineering Services Corporation, now turned nuclear whistle-blower, once a zirconium fire has started, due to its extreme temperatures and high degree of reactivity, contact with water will result in the water dissociating into hydrogen and oxygen gases, which will almost certainly lead to violent explosions. Gundersen says that once a zirconium fuel rod fire has started, the worst thing you could do is to try to quench the fire with water streams, since this action will only make matters worse and lead to violent explosions. Gundersen believes the massive explosion that blew the roof off the spent fuel pond at Fukushima was caused by zirconium induced hydrogen dissociation[16].

A few days after the tidal waves destroyed the generators providing back-up electrical power to Fukushima Daiichi's cooling system, the protective water bath boiled away from the spent fuel pond for reactor no. 4, leaving the stored spent fuel rods partially exposed to the air. Had it not been for heroic efforts on the part of Japan's nuclear workers to replenish water in this spent fuel pool, these spent rods would have melted down and their zirconium cladding would have ignited, which most likely would have released far more radioactive contamination than what came from the three reactor core meltdowns.

Japanese officials estimate that, to date, the Fukushima Daiichi nuclear disaster has released just over half of the total radioactive contamination released from Chernobyl, but other sources suggest that the radiation released could be significantly more. In the event of an extreme GMD-induced long-term grid collapse covering much of the globe, if just half of the world's spent fuel ponds boil off their water and become radioactive zirconium-fed infernos, the ensuing contamination will far exceed the cumulative effect of 400 Chernobyls.

Most of us tend to believe that a nuclear reactor is something that can be shut down in short order, like some massive piece of machinery that can be turned off by simply flipping a switch, or by performing a series of operations in a prescribed manner over a relatively short time, such as a few hours or perhaps a day or two. In spite of my MIT education (BSME, MIT, 1978), until recently I too was under the spell of this comforting delusion, which is far from the truth. You see, the trillions of chain reactions going on inside a nuclear reactor's core continuously produce such incredible amounts of energy that a single nuclear power plant can generate more electricity than is required to power a good sized city. Unfortunately, these reactions do not simply "cease fire" at the flip of a switch. In general, it takes 5 to 7 days to slow down a reactor core's nuclear chain reactions to the point where the core may be removed from the reactor.

After removal, the fuel rods are quite "hot", both from the perspective of temperature and radioactivity. For the next 3 to 5 years these fuel rods must be immersed under roughly 20 feet of continuously cooled water, both to shield the surrounding area from radioactivity, as well as to prevent catastrophic melt-down from occurring. According to Gundersen, after slowing down the chain reactions inside the reactor cores at Fukushima for a full eight months, the fuel rods would start melting down again if coolant flow was suspended for just 38 hours.

Gundersen explained that, essentially all modern nuclear reactors are designed with banks of "fuel rods", which contain highly radioactive materials, combined with banks of "control rods", which mesh between the fuel rods like the interwoven fingers of your right and left hands. It is the degree of interweave that moderates and controls the rate of nuclear chain reactions. He further explained that in the event of a significant loss of reactor control, reactors are designed for a "fail-safe" process to occur, where the control rods automatically fall into the fully meshed position with respect to the fuel rods, resulting in maximal slowing of the core's nuclear reactions and beginning the process of shutting down the reactor.

Typically, this action rapidly reduces the power produced by these chain reactions by a factor of 20:1 (to 5.0 per cent of full power), but that still leaves thousands of horsepower worth of waste heat that must be removed if the reactor core is not to rapidly overheat and fail catastrophically. After a day of leaving the control rods in the fully interwoven position, this reaction slows to 1.0 per cent, and after a week it will be about 0.1 per cent of full power. Once the reactions in the fuel rods slow to the point where the rods may be removed from the reactor, the spent fuel rods must be cooled inside containment ponds for 3–5 more years before the nuclear reactions decay to a point where the rods can be moved to specially designed air-cooled storage banks.

As mentioned previously, nuclear power plants are only required to store enough backup fuel reserves on-site to keep their backup diesel generators running for a period of one week. The NRC has always operated from the assumption that extended grid "blackouts" would not last for periods of more than a few days. The government has promised that, in the event of a major catastrophe such as a Hurricane Katrina, diesel trucks will show up like clockwork at all troubled nuclear facilities until local grid-supplied electrical power services have been re-established. Unfortunately, governments and regulators have not considered the possibility that the next extreme GMD which Mother Nature unleashes upon Earth will quite likely disrupt grid services over much of the industrial world for a period of years, not just days. The chances that the world's nuclear reactors will receive weekly deliveries of diesel fuel under such chaotic circumstances are practically zero. In a world suffering from loss of fuel and electric power, if any such deliveries were attempted those fuel tankers would be prime targets for armed hijackers. *(Continued on Page 8)*

When Disaster Strikes

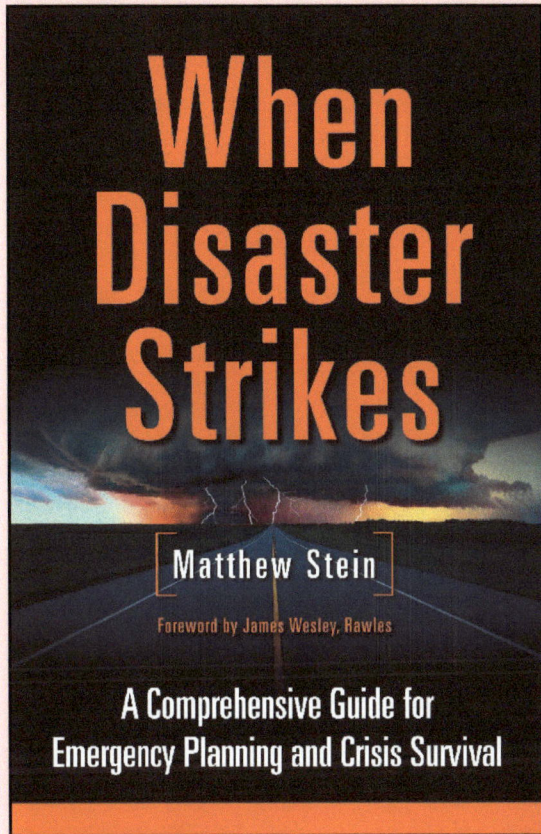

Disasters often strike without warning and leave a trail of destruction in their wake. Yet armed with the right tools and information, survivors can fend for themselves and get through even the toughest circumstances. Matthew Stein's When Disaster Strikes provides a thorough, practical guide for how to prepare for and react in many of life's most unpredictable scenarios.

In this disaster-preparedness manual, he outlines the materials you'll need-from food and water, to shelter and energy, to first-aid and survival skills-to help you safely live through the worst. When Disaster Strikes covers how to find and store food, water, and clothing, as well as the basics of installing back-up power and lights. You'll learn how to gather and sterilize water, build a fire, treat injuries in an emergency, and use alternative medical sources when conventional ones are unavailable.

Stein instructs you on the smartest responses to natural disasters-such as fires, earthquakes, hurricanes and floods-how to keep warm during winter storms, even how to protect yourself from attack or other dangerous situations. With this comprehensive guide in hand, you can be sure to respond quickly, correctly, and confidently when a crisis threatens.

Author, engineer, designer, and green builder, Mat Stein was born and raised in Burlington Vermont. His parents started him walking on skis at age three, hiking at age 5, backpacking at age seven, hunting at age 10, rock climbing and extreme skiing at age 11. The Green mountains of Vermont, White mountains of New Hampshire, and the Adirondack's of upstate New York were his four-season childhood play grounds. After graduating from MIT in 1978, where he majored in Mechanical Engineering, the lure of the "real mountains" of the west drew Mat across the country to California.

A thirty year interest in alternative healing got its start while Mat was still a freshman at MIT, when he witnessed the miraculous remote healing of a crippled friend (big shake up to his scientific "Billiard Ball Theory of the Universe" way of thinking). Over the years, this interest expanded to the use of herbs, homeopathy, and other alternatives to heal medical conditions that weren't responding to western style medicine.

The engineer, carpenter, and backwoodsman sides of Mat found peace, harmony, and synergy through renewable energy, green building, and self-reliance. Today, Mat owns and operates Stein Design and Construction, providing product design services, engineering analysis, and green building.

It was a true epiphany that started Mat firmly on the path of self-reliance, emergency prep, and sustainability. Around Thanksgiving of 1997, during his morning session of prayer and meditation, in answer to a simple request for "guidance and inspiration", Mat received a fully developed "story board" type of pictorial outline that popped into his head instantaneously. It was the outline for a massive handbook to help people be more self-reliant, live more sustainably, and prepare to weather the coming storms as we pass through this age of uncertainty and change. After three years of work, this "cosmic download" crystallized into his first book, When Technology Fails.

Stein has appeared on numerous radio and television programs and is a repeat guest on Fox News, MSNBC, Lionel, The 'X' Zone Radio Show, Coast-to-Coast AM, and the Thom Hartmann Show. For more information, visit Mat's websites listed below.

When Disaster Strikes is Available at Amazon.com

400 Chernobyls:
Solar Flares, EMP, and Nuclear Armageddon
Continued From Page 6

Had it not been for heroic efforts on the part of Japan's nuclear workers to replenish waters in the spent fuel pool at Fukushima, those spent fuel rods would have melted down and ignited their zirconium cladding, which most likely would have released far more radioactive contamination than what came from the three reactor core melt-downs. Japanese officials have estimate that the Fukushima Daiichi nuclear disaster has already released into the local environment just over half the total radioactive contamination as was released by Chernobyl, but other sources estimate it could be significantly more than was released by the accident at Chernobyl. In the event that an extreme GMD induced long-term grid collapse covering much of the globe, if just half of the world's spent fuel ponds were to boil off their water and become radioactive zirconium fed infernos, the ensuing contamination could far exceed the cumulative effect of 400 Chernobyls.

Electromagnetic Pulse (EMP) Attack

Many of the control systems we considered achieved optimal connectivity through Ethernet cabling. EMP coupling of electrical transients to the cables proved to be an important vulnerability during threat illumination.... The testing and analysis indicate that the electronics could be expected to see roughly 100 to 700 ampere current transients on typical Ethernet cables. Effects noted in EMP testing occurred at the lower end of this scale. The bottom line observation at the end of the testing was that every system failed when exposed to the simulated EMP environment.

— Report of the Commission to Asses the Threat to the United States from Electromagnetic Pulse (EMP) Attack[18]

Electromagnetic pulses (EMPs) and solar super storms are two different, but related, categories of events that are often described as high-impact, low frequency (HILF) events. Events categorized as HILF don't happen very often, but if and when they do they have the potential to severely affect the lives of many millions of people. Think of an EMP as a super-powerful radio wave capable of inducing damaging voltage spikes in electrical wires and electronic devices across vast geographical areas. What is generally referred to as an EMP strike is the deliberate detonation of a nuclear device at a high altitude, roughly defined as somewhere between 24 and 240 miles (40 and 400 kilometers) above the surface of the earth. Nuclear detonations of this type have the potential to cause serious damage to electronics and electrical power grids along their line of sight, covering huge distances on the order of a circular area 1,500 miles (2,500 kilometers) in diameter, which would correspond to an area stretching roughly from Quebec City in Canada down to Dallas, Texas and reaching almost as far south as Miami, Florida. The geomagnetic

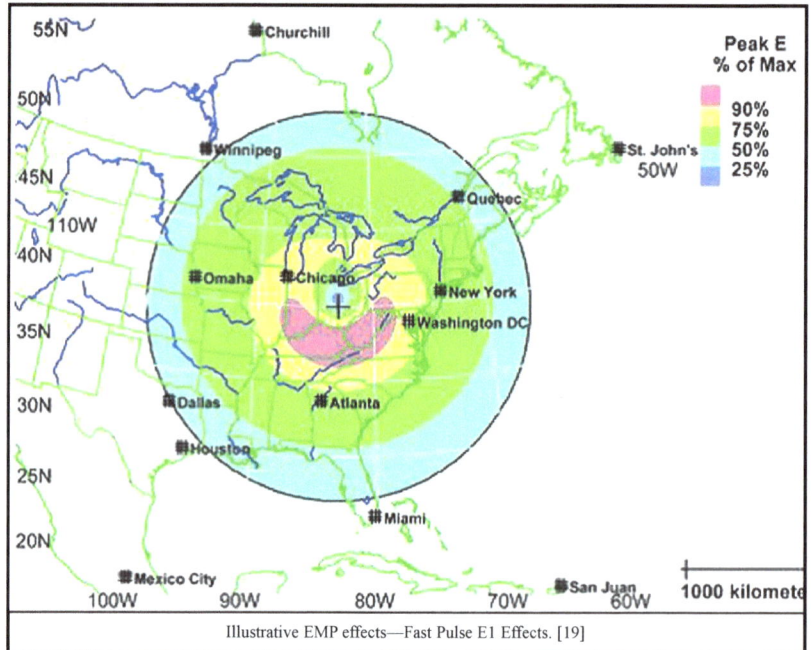

Illustrative EMP effects—Fast Pulse E1 Effects. [19]

effects of extreme solar storms are sometimes also described as a "natural EMP".

The concern is that some rogue state or terrorist organization might build their own nuclear device from scratch or buy one illegally, procure a Scud missile (or similar) on the black market and launch their nuclear device from a large fishing boat or freighter somewhere off the coast of the US, causing grid collapse and widespread damage to electronic devices across roughly 50% of America. Much like an extreme GMD, a powerful EMP attack would also cause widespread grid collapse, but it would be limited to a much smaller geographical area.

A powerful EMP from a sub-orbital nuclear detonation would cause extreme electromagnetic effects, starting with an initial short duration "speed of light" pulse, referred to as an "E1" effect, followed by a middle duration pulse called an "E2" effect, which is followed by a longer duration disturbance known as an "E3" effect. The "E1" effect lasts on the order of a few nanoseconds, and is quite similar to massive electrostatic discharges, much like the sparks that surge from an extended fingertip after rubbing your feet on the carpet on a cold clear winter's day, except they would surge through the hearts of electronic equipment distributed over a vast geographic area. These types of electrostatic spark discharges are particularly damaging to digital microelectronic chips that are at the core of most modern electronic equipment.

The intermediate "E2" effects last a fraction of a second, and are similar to many thousands to millions of lightning strikes hitting over a widespread area at almost exactly the same time. Unfortunately, many of the devices designed to protect equipment from lightning damage, such as surge protectors, will be incapacitated by damage from the E1 pulse, leaving millions of electronic devices and systems susceptible to damage from the E2 effects.

In the case of a nuclear induced EMP, its E3 effect starts after about a half second and may continue for several minutes. The E3 effect

can be thought of as a "long slow burn", and electromagnetically it is quite similar to the effects from an extreme GMD. The main difference between the E3 from an EMP and what occurs during an extreme GMD is that the EMP effect may continue for a number of minutes, whereas the extreme GMD may continue for a number of hours or days. However, the magnitude of the induced magnetic field strengths from an EMP attack and an extreme GMD are about the same, with similar potential for causing severe damage to EHV transformers across the affected areas.

Inside the affected area, an EMP's E3 effect would cause a similar degree of damage to the EHV transformers as that from an extreme GMD, but the E1 and E2 effects would cause far greater damage to electronic control systems than that from a GMD of similar intensity. Contrary to popular opinion, most personal electronic devices would probably survive with little or no damage, especially if they were not turned on at the moment of EMP, as would most automobiles. However, most complex electronic systems that contained digital microchips in combination with long runs of Ethernet cables (or other interconnecting cabling) which act like antennas for receiving EMP induced voltage spikes, would experience nearly 100% failure! [20]

(Continued on Page 9)

400 Chernobyls:

Solar Flares, EMP, and Nuclear Armageddon

Continued From Page 8

A "successful" EMP attack launched against the US would most likely result in the immediate collapse of the grid across roughly 50% of the country, and crash the stock market. For the reasons discussed above, modern digital electronic control systems are highly susceptible to damage from EMP. These systems include programmable logic controllers (PLC), digital control systems (DCS), and supervisory control and data acquisition systems (SCADA), all of which are absolutely critical for running factories, refineries, power plants, nuclear reactors, sewage plants, etc., as well as for diagnosing problems within those facilities and systems.

Bill Kaewert, President and CTO of Stored Energy Systems, LLC, a supplier of backup power systems and components for mission-critical structures, such as Minuteman III missile silos, data centers, and critical corporate facilities, recently took part in a "Tabletop EMP" exercise hosted at the National Defense University. Dozens of the nation's leading first responders, public safety experts, and military personnel took part in this exercise simulating a massive grid-down scenario typical of an EMP attack or an extreme GMD. According to Kaewert, even these highly trained personnel had a hard time grappling with the public safety implications of a disaster the size of fifty Hurricane Katrinas. It was also quite apparent that in an extended grid collapse a large number of emergency responders, military and government personnel would abandon their posts to protect their family and friends from the ensuing chaos[21].

In October of 1962, the Soviet Union conducted three above ground nuclear tests over Kazahhstan to study the effects of EMP. Due to its more northerly location, the EMP effects at the Kazahhstan test site were several times stronger than those observed during the more well known "Starfish Prime" nuclear test, where the U.S. military detonated a 1.4 megaton nuclear device in July of 1962, 250 miles above Johnston Island, which is 900 miles south of Honolulu, HI. During the Soviet EMP tests, massive current spikes were induced in a 600 mile (1000 kilometer) long high-voltage power line that was buried six feet (two meters) underground. Massive induced currents caused a fire in the Karaganda power plant at the far end of the line, burning it to the ground. In anticipation of power outages caused by the EMP tests, the Russian military had preplaced a backup diesel generators on site, but many of these generators were damaged by the EMP blast and would not start prior to being repaired. Located at great distances from the test site ground zero, several military radar units were also disabled by the EMP. Due to the use of solid-state devices containing microchips, today's electrical devices are generally far less resistant to EMP damage than the devices in use during these EMP tests that took place back in the early 1960's. In today's world, scientists

predict that within the heavily affected area an EMP strike would cripple many backup power systems along with the vast majority of digital electronic control systems.

Since his deployment with the U.S. military in the early 1980's, Dr. George Baker has been involved the study of EMP effects, as well as the design of EMP hardened devices, EMP weapons, and developing EMP standards for military and civilian usage. His resume reads like a "Who's Who" of EMP, including being a Principal Staff member of the Congressional Commission to Asses the Threat to the United States from Electromagnetic Pulse (EMP). Baker states that, "electronic systems are so complex, from an electromagnetic coupling standpoint, that we simply cannot predict what will fail or survive an EMP event. Actual EMP testing is the only way to know whether or not a particular electronic device will survive an EMP attack." [22]

The only good news about EMP strike is that its effect will cover a much smaller area than an extreme GMD, so there will be a significant portion of the rest of the US, as well as the rest of the outside world, left intact and able to lend a hand towards rebuilding critical infrastructure in the affected areas. Imagine the near total loss of a functioning infrastructure across an area of about a million square miles (approximately 1.6 million square kilometers, roughly equivalent to 50 Hurricane Katrinas happening simultaneously) and you will have some idea of the crippling effect of an EMP attack from a single medium sized sub-orbital nuclear detonation!

The simple fact of the matter is that approximately 1/3 of the population of the U.S. lives within 50 miles of a nuclear power plant, the vast majority of which are located in the eastern half of the country—the prime target for an EMP attack. If the reactor vessel was breeched at the Indian Point nuclear power plant 38 mile north of New York City, and the city itself was contaminated with four times the safe level of Cesium 137 (a radioactive isotope that was deposited at dangerous levels on areas surrounding Fukushima), which has a half life of 30 years, then it would take roughly 60 years before the local Cesium 137 decayed to levels at which New York City could be safely re-occupied[23]. Given the likelihood that backup power systems will fail at a significant percentage of the nuclear installations within the EMP affected area, and the distinct probability that all utilities and central services would collapse over many of the nation's population centers, the need to invest in preventative measures should be quite obvious.

Preventing Armageddon

The congressionally mandated EMP Commission has studied the threat of both EMP and extreme GMD events, and made recommendations to the US congress to implement protective devices and procedures to insure the survival of the grid and other critical infrastructures in either event. John Kappenman, author of the Metatech study, in a February 2012 IEEE Journal article, A Perfect Storm of Planetary Proportions, discusses various technologies that have been recently developed to protect to grid from severe geomagnetic disturbances. Kappenman

estimates that it would cost on the order of $1 billion to build special protective devices into the US grid to protect its EHV transformers from EMP or extreme GMD damage, and to build stores of critical replacement parts should some of these items be damaged or destroyed. Kappenman estimates that it would cost significantly less than $1 billion to store at least a year's worth of diesel fuel for backup generators at each US nuclear facility and to store sets of critical spare parts, such as backup generators, inside EMP-hardened steel containers to be available for quick change-out in the event that any of these items were damaged by an EMP or GMD[24].

To me, this is a no-brainer. For the cost of a single B-2 bomber or a tiny fraction of the TARP bank bailout, we could invest in preventative measures to avert what might well become the end of our civilization and life as we know it! There is no way to protect against all possible effects from an extreme GMD or an EMP attack, but certainly we could implement measures to protect against the worst effects. Since 2008, Congress has narrowly failed to pass legislation that would implement at least some of the EMP Commission's recommendations[25].

For more than 50 years, the US Army Corps of Engineers knew that New Orleans was a disaster waiting to happen, and they made plans for rebuilding the aging system of inadequate levies, but those plans were never implemented. Have we learned nothing from the wholly preventable flooding of New Orleans? Will we continue to ignore facts and pretend that "everything will be OK" while our world drifts towards the next inevitable extreme GMD, or until some terrorist organization or rogue state launches an EMP attack? This time, failure to prepare will not just mean the loss of a major city, but the end of the industrialized world as we know it, along with incalculable suffering, death, and environmental destruction.

We have a long ways to go to make our world EMP and GMD safe. Every citizen can do their part to push for legislation to move towards this goal, and to work inside our homes and communities to develop local resilience and self reliance, so that in the event of a long term grid-down scenario, we might make the most of a bad situation. The same tools that are espoused by the "Transition Movement" for developing local self-reliance and resilience to help cope with the twin effects of climate change and peak oil could also serve communities well in the event of an EMP attack or extreme GMD. If our country were to implement safeguards to protect our grid and nuclear power plants from EMP, it would also eliminate the primary incentive for a terrorist to launch an EMP attack. The sooner we take these actions the less chance that an EMP attack will occur!

For more information, or to get involved, see http://empactamerica.org/, http://survive-emp.com/, and http://www.transitionnetwork.org/ or contact your congressman at http://www.contactingthecongress.org/.

(Continued on Page 10)

400 Chernobyls:
Solar Flares, EMP, and Nuclear Armageddon
Continued From Page 9

NOTES:

[1] Bill Dedman, "Nuclear Neighbors: Population Rises Near Nuclear Reactors," MSNBC.com. Available at http://www.msnbc.msn.com/id/42555888/ns/us_news-life/t/nuclear-neighbors-population-rises-near-us-reactors/#. Accessed December 2011.

[2] Dina Cappiello, "Long Blackouts Pose Risk to U.S. Nuclear Reactors," Associated Press, March 29, 2011.

[3] Lawrence E. Joseph, "The Sun Also Surprises," New York Times, August 15, 2010. Available at http://www.nytimes.com/2010/08/16/opinion/16joseph.html. Accessed August 2010.

[4] John Kappenman, "Geomagnetic Storms and Their Impacts on the U.S. Power Grid," Metatech Corporation, prepared for Oak Ridge National Laboratory, Meta-R-319, January 2010, p. 2—29.

[5] S. M. Silverman and E. W. Cliver, "Low-Altitude Auroras: The Magnetic Storm of 14-15 May 1921," Journal of Atmospheric and Solar-Terrestrial Physics 63, (2001), p. 523-535. Additionally, "High-Impact, Low-Frequency Event Risk to the North American Bulk Power System: A Jointly Commissioned Summary Report of the North American Electric Reliability Corporation and the U.S. Department of Energy's November 2009 Workshop," June, 2010, p. 68.

[6] Committee on the Societal and Economic Impacts of Severe Space Weather Events: A Workshop National Research Council, "Severe Space Weather Events: Understanding Societal and Economic Impacts Workshop Report," National Research Council of the National Academies (2008), p. 7-13, and p. 100. Additionally, E. W. Cliver and L. Svalgaard, "The 1859 Solar-Terrestrial Disturbance and the Current Limits of Extreme Space Weather Activity," Solar Physics (2004) 224, P. 407-422.

[7] Richard A. Lovett, "What if the Biggest Solar Storm on Record Happened Today?" National Geographic News, March 2, 2011. Available at http://news.nationalgeographic.com/news/2011/03/110302-solar-flares-sun-storms-earth-danger-carrington-event-science/. Accessed December 2011.

[8] John Kappenman, "Geomagnetic Storms and Their Impacts on the U.S. Power Grid," Metatech Corporation, prepared for Oak Ridge National Laboratory, Meta-R-319, January 2010. Available at http://www.ornl.gov/sci/ees/etsd/pes/pubs/ferc_Meta-R-319.pdf. Accessed November 2011.

[9] Ibid., p. 1—3.

[10] Ibid., p. 4—2.

[11] John Kappenman, interview by author, December 2011.

[12] "Sagging Power Lines, Hot Weather Blamed for Blackout," CNN News, August 11, 1996. Available at http://www.cnn.com/US/9608/11/power.outage. Accessed June 2000.

[13] Bryan Walsh, "Can We Prevent Another Blackout?" Time, August 11, 2008. Available at http://www.time.com/time/health/article/0,8599,1831346,00.html. Accessed December 2011.

[14] Lauren Effron, David Wright, Julie NA and Jason Volack, "One Electrical Worker Blamed for Leaving Millions Without Power in California, Arizona, and Mexico," ABC News, September 8, 2011. Available at http://abcnews.go.com/US/electrical-worker-blamed-leaving-millions-power-california-arizona/story?id=14478198#.TuGjBPKGCJs. Accessed December 2011.

[15] John Vidal, "Nuclear's Green Cheerleaders Forget Chernobyl at Our Peril," Guardian.co.uk, April 1, 2011. Available at http://www.guardian.co.uk/commentisfree/2011/apr/01/fukushima-chernobyl-risks-radiation. Accessed May 2011.

[16] NUREG-1738, "Technical Study of Spent Fuel Pool Accident Risk at Decommissioning Nuclear Power Plants," February 2001, as reported in "Petition for Rulemaking: Docket No. PRM-50-96," Foundation for Resilient Societies before the Nuclear Regulatory Commission, p. 3-9 and 49-50. Available at http://www.resilientsocieties.org/images/Petition_For_Rulemaking_Resilient_Societies_Docketed.pdf. Accessed December, 2011.

[17] Arnold Gundersen, interview by author, November 2011.

[18] "Report of the Commission to Assess the Threat to the United States from Electromagnetic Pulse (EMP) Attack: Critical National Infrastructures," April, 2008, p. 6.

[19] "Report of the Commission to Assess the Threat to the United States from Electromagnetic Pulse (EMP) Attack: Volume 1: Executive Report," 2004, p. 6.

[20] "Report of the Commission to Assess the Threat to the United States from Electromagnetic Pulse (EMP) Attack: Critical National Infrastructures," April, 2008. Extensively referred to for EMP definitions and effects.

[21] Bill Kaewert, interview by author, December 2011.

[22] Dr. George Baker, interview by author, December 2011

[23] Victor Gilinsky, "Indian Point: The Next Fukushima?" The New York Times, December 16, 2011. Available at http://www.nytimes.com/2011/12/17/opinion/is-indian-point-the-next-fukushima.html. Accessed December 2011.

[24] John Kappenman, interview by author, December 2011. Also John Kappenman, "A Perfect Storm of Planetary Proportions" IEEE Spectrum, February, 2012. Available at http://spectrum.ieee.org/energy/the-smarter-grid/a-perfect-storm-of-planetary-proportions/0

[25] Dr. Peter Vincent Pry, "Statement Before the Congressional Caucus on EMP," EMPact America, February 15, 2011. Available at http://www.empactamerica.org/pry-statement-to-emp-caucus.pdf. Accessed November 2011.

Additional references not directly cited:

"Nuke Plant's Generator Failures Draw Scrutiny," CBS News, October 10, 2011. Available at http://www.cbsnews.com/stories/2011/10/10/national/main20118118.shtml. Accessed December 2011.

Gary Null, PhD, and Jeremy Stillman, "Solar Storms: Katrina Times 1000? A Real Armageddon Meltdown is Possible," Progressive Radio Network, October 6, 2011. Available at http://www.garynull.com/home/gary-null-phd-and-jeremy-stillman-solar-storms-katrina-times.html Beth Daley, "Markey: Back-Up Generators Failed During Tests at US Nuclear Power Plants," Boston Globe, May 12, 2011. Available at http://www.boston.com/lifestyle/green/greenblog/2011/05/markey_back-up_generators_fail.html. Accessed Jan 2012.

Yousaf M. Butt, "The EMP Threat: Fact, Fiction, and Response (Part 1)," The Space Review, January 25, 2010. Available at http://www.thespacereview.com/article/1549/2. Accessed December 2012.

Yousaf M. Butt, "The EMP Threat: Fact, Fiction, and Response (Part 2)," The Space Review, January 25, 2010. Available at http://www.thespacereview.com/article/1553/1. Accessed December 2012.

"Initial Economic Assessment of Electromagnetic Pulse (EMP) Impact Upon the Baltimore-Richmond Region," by The Sage Policy Group, September 10, 2007. Available at http://survive-emp.com/fileadmin/White-Papers/EMP-Resources/EMP-Econ-Study.pdf. Accessed December 2011.

Edward Savage, James Gilbert, and William Radasky, "Early-Time (E1) High-Altitude Electromagnetic Pulse (HEMP) and Its Impact on the U.S. Power Grid," Metatech Corporation, prepared for Oak Ridge National Laboratory, Meta-R-320, January 2010. Available at http://www.ornl.gov/sci/ees/etsd/pes/pubs/ferc_Meta-R-320.pdf. Accessed January 2012.

James Gilbert, John Kappenman, William Radasky, and Edward Savage, "The Late-Time (E3) High-Altitude Electromagnetic Pulse (HEMP) and Its Impact on the U.S. Power Grid," Metatech Corporation, prepared for Oak Ridge National Laboratory, Meta-R-321, January 2010. Available at http://www.ornl.gov/sci/ees/etsd/pes/pubs/ferc_Meta-R-321.pdf. Accessed January 2012.

About the author:

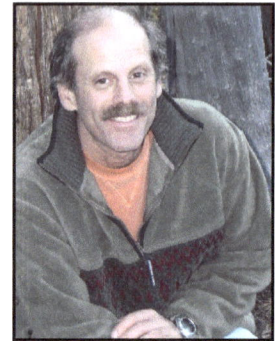

Matthew Stein is a design engineer, green builder, and author of two bestselling books: When Disaster Strikes: A Comprehensive Guide to Emergency Planning and Crisis Survival (Chelsea Green 2011), and When Technology Fails: A Manual for Self-Reliance, Sustainability, and Surviving the Long Emergency (Chelsea Green 2008). Stein is a graduate of the Massachusetts Institute of Technology (MIT) where he majored in Mechanical Engineering. Stein has appeared on numerous radio and television programs and is a repeat guest on Fox News, Lionel, Coast-to-Coast AM, The 'X' Zone Radio/TV Show and the Thom Hartmann Show. He is an active mountain climber, serves as a guide and instructor for blind skiers, has written several articles on the subject of sustainable living, and is a guest columnist for the Huffington Post. []

UFO SIGHTINGS CHART ONE

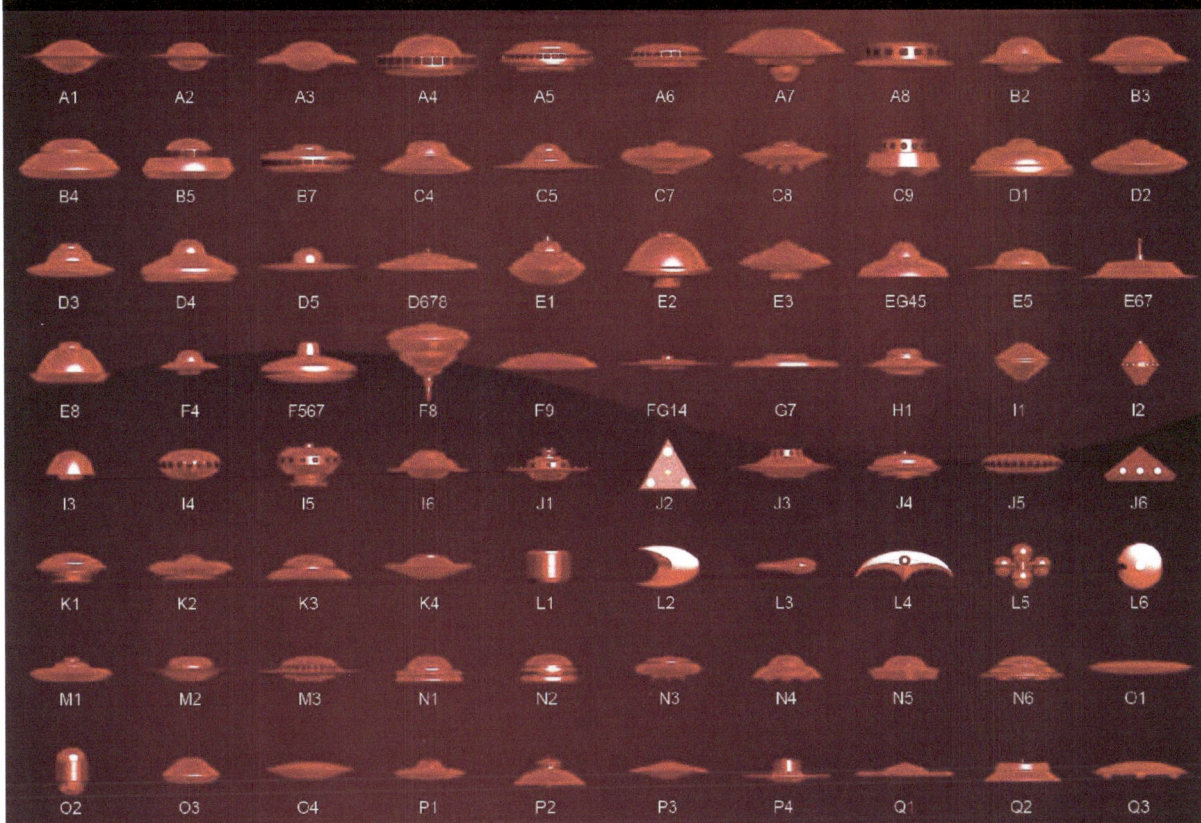

A1	A2	A3	A4	A5	A6	A7	A8	B2	B3
B4	B5	B7	C4	C5	C7	C8	C9	D1	D2
D3	D4	D5	D678	E1	E2	E3	EG45	E5	E67
E8	F4	F567	F8	F9	FG14	G7	H1	I1	I2
I3	I4	I5	I6	J1	J2	J3	J4	J5	J6
K1	K2	K3	K4	L1	L2	L3	L4	L5	L6
M1	M2	M3	N1	N2	N3	N4	N5	N6	O1
O2	O3	O4	P1	P2	P3	P4	Q1	Q2	Q3

UFOs Through The Ages

People have been seeing strange objects in the sky since the beginning of recorded history. The fiery clouds and burning globes of biblical times gave way in the 20th century to airships, futuristic planes, and "ghost rockets."

The modern era of the UFO is usually presumed to have begun in the summer of 1947. On June 24 of that year, a pilot from Idaho by the name of Kenneth Arnold reported nine silvery, crescent-shaped objects skimming at high speed over the jagged peaks of the cascade Range in Washington state. Arnold later described their motion as like that "of a saucer skipping over water." An Associated Press reporter shortened the phrase to "flying saucers," and the rest, as they say is history.

The heavens, it appears, have always been haunted by UFO's, or at least since there have been human observers to record them. The French ufologist and author Aime Michel, for example, points to a series of Paleolithic Cro-Magnon cave paintings scattered throughout Europe that date to about 20,000 B.C. Some appear to portray objects similar in the shape to the Apollo module that first landed American astronauts on the moon, complete with antenna and landing struts. Among the bison, deer, and mammoths on the famous Altamira cave paintings in Spain are similar saucers, at least one with what seems to be a figure standing alongside. Are these crude line drawings the first evidence of extraterrestrial visitors? Or are they merely the artistic rendering of ancient magical symbols?

Raining fishes and birds

An Egyptian papyrus, said to be a 3,400-year-old fragment of the Annals of Thutmose III, may contain the first written account of a UFO. The papyrus describes numerous nocturnal "fire circles" that "shone more in the sky than he brightness of the sun." Rising high in the south, the fiery circles rained down "fishes and winged creatures…a marvel never before known since the foundation of land." The pharaoh ordered incense burned, and the event recorded for future posterity.

The two great epic religious poems of India, the Mahabharata and Ramayana, written more than 2,000 years ago, both mention disc-like military flying machines called vimanas. Another ancient Indian manuscript, dealing mostly with matters of town planning and architecture, gives matter-of-fact instructions for the manufacture of various vimanas, although the precise meaning of specific steps and materials of certain chemical formulas remains ambiguous. The vimanas has extraordinary destructive potential, similar to today's nuclear weapons, and leveling of the city of Varanasi is described in fearsome detail.

In Genesis 19:24-28 brimstone and fire rained out of the heavens to cause the utter destruction of Sodom and Gomorrah. Equally striking is the strange spectacle of a fiery cloud recorded by the prophet Ezekiel around 600 B.C. Various interpretations of this event have been offered over the years, two rarely alike because of the obscure imagery employed. But Ezekiel's experience is not unlike that reported by later UFO contactees and abductees. He was lifted aboard this strange craft by a spirit force, and then carried away to another world.

The Romans of more recent antiquity also recorded sightings of unexplained objects in the sky. The Roman writers Livy and Pliny each report a mysterious fiery object falling toward the earth, in 214 B.C. and 66 B.C. respectively. Julius Obsequens, who was writing in the fourth century A.D., speaks of witnesses who had seen several round shields and burning globes both by day and night in the skies above or near Rome. Medieval chroniclers echo these reports. A famous woodcut by Hans Glaser bears graphic witness to a war waged in the heavens above Nuremburg, Germany, on April 14, 1561. During the early morning hours, the skies were filled with cylindrical UFO's, from which emerged numerous black, red, and orange globes or smoking spheres. A similar event, also captured in woodcut, seems to have taken place above Basel, Switzerland, on August 7, 1577. This time large numbers of black spheres appeared to be engaged in a furious battle.

(Continued On Page 12)

UFOs Through The Ages
Continued From Page 11

What were our ancestors seeing? Like the biblical prophets, people in the Middle Ages tended to interpret these aerial phantoms as religious portents. The possibility always remains, of course, that they were simply misrepresenting ordinary atmospheric phenomena such as meteors and the aurora Borealis, or northern lights. The possibility also exists that they were witnessing something truly anomalous. And as we shall see, strikingly similar sights have been reported by more modern observers as well.

Beginning in the autumn of 1896, Californians in San Francisco, Oakland, and Sacramento claimed hundreds of sightings of what soon became known as the Great Airship. By the following spring reports were more numerous and widespread.

Time and time again, witnesses told tales of a large cigar-shaped object moving slowly through the night skies. Some saw huge membranes like the wings of a giant insect, lighted portholes, and obscure shadows that moved about the superstructure. Others reported the chugging sound of motors, and a brilliant ray that beamed downward. It was sometimes encountered on the ground, usually in some sort of difficulty, and manned by a foreign crew. So persistent were such reports that the father of the light bulb, Thomas Alva Edison, felt compelled to call a press conference to deny that he had invented the Great Airship.

The age of aviation

In early May 1897, the sightings stopped. Skeptics claim the entire episode was nothing more than a magnificent hoax, engineered by bored railroad telegraphers and sensationalized by the popular press. Other regard the Great Airship as a precursor, physical or psychological, of things to come. A few years later, in 1903, the Wright brothers lifted a heavier-than-air contraption off the sand dunes at Kitty Hawk, North Carolina, and overnight the world entered a new age. Now we too could soar with the birds, perhaps in time as far as the sun and the other stars. But for the moment our anonymous aerial visitors remained one step ahead.

A cigar-shaped craft

In 1909 the Airship was back, this time over England, and with a more modern, faster design. The case reported by police constable Kettle of Peterborough, near Cambridge, is typical. In the early morning hours of March 23, 1909, his attention was drawn to the "steady buzz of a high-powered engine." Kettle next observed "a powerful light," which he estimated "to have been some 1,200 feet above the ground." He also saw a "dark body, oblong and narrow in shape, outlined against the stars... it was travelling at a tremendous pace, and as I watched, the rattle of the engines gradually grew fainter."

There were hundreds of reports of a whirring sound from above, a cigar-shaped craft, and a brilliant light beaming groundward.

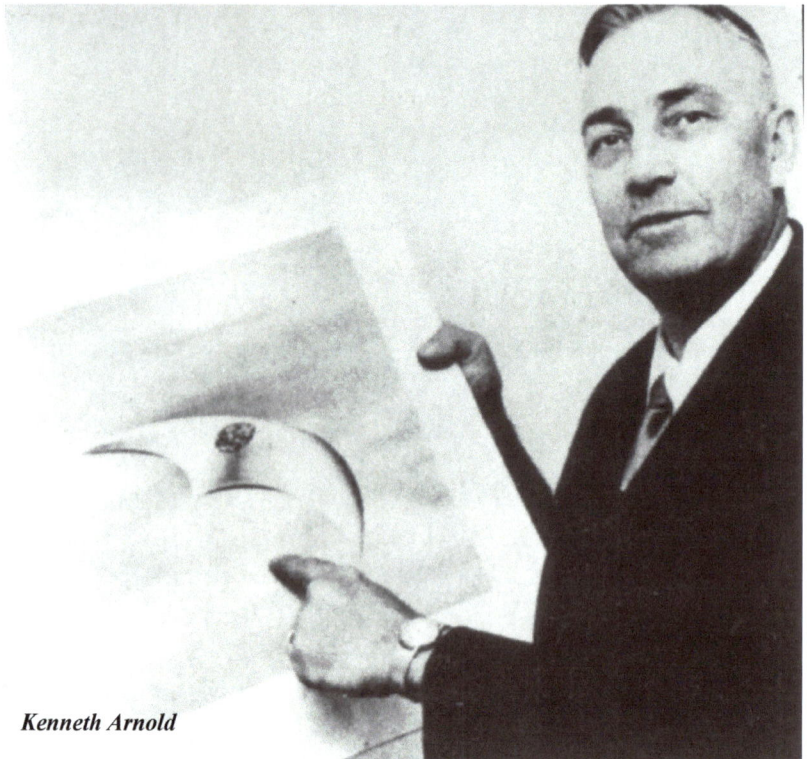

Kenneth Arnold

What is apparent is that there were not nearly enough real airships in the world to explain all these sightings. The Germans, for example, had only three Zeppelins operational at the time. But up to and even after the outbreak of hostilities in 1914, northern Europe would be plagued by such reports. The Danes blamed the British, who suspected the Germans, who in turn accused the British. But the mysterious craft did not cause any trouble - they seemed to be passive observers of the turmoil below.

The period between the World Wars was not without incident either. From 1933 until 1938, Norway, Sweden, and Finland were inundated with reports of the "Ghost-flier." Unlike its predecessors, the Ghost-flier was reported as a large airplane, with ordinary wings, nose, and tail. This phantom plane performed the patently impossible, flying at low altitude over treacherous mountain terrain in snow and fog. Its arrival was often announced by a brilliant beam of light.

Foo fighters

Public apprehension was so aroused by press reports that systematic expeditions were organized in search of Russian or German "spy bases" suspected of harbouring the mysterious plane. Nothing was found, but two army plane crashes among the fjords and one navy cruiser ran aground in the search. Less than a year later, Hitler's Blitzkrieg overran Poland. Suddenly, there was a new, totally terrestrial ogre to contend with, more malignant that any visitor from the planet Mars. But even the ensuing worldwide conflict could not conceal the fact that UFO's were still invading our planet's night skies. The latest UFO manifestation quickly became known as "foo fighters." He origin of the phrase itself remains uncertain, but it seems to have stemmed from the comic Smokey Stover, which was popular among GI's. One of its catchphrases was" "Where there's a foo, there's fire!" ("Foo" was probably a corruption of the French word for fire, feu, with additional overtones of fou, meaning crazy.)

Foo fighters commonly materialized as small luminous balls of various-coloured light, predominantly orange, green, and white. They appeared both at night and in the daytime, and were reported as playing tag with Allied fighters and bombers in both the Pacific and European theatres of operations.

Ghost rockets

The sightings of unknown aerial objects did not cease with the end of the war. No sooner had the mushroom clouds over Hiroshima and Nagasaki evaporated than Sweden began reporting strange "ghost rockets." These objects resembled the V-1 and V-2 rockets that rained death and destruction on wartime London.

Despite the fact that the ghost rockets were photographed on several occasions and more than a thousand cases in all were catalogued, there was no satisfactory explanation. And, after a brief spate of convincing reports, the ghost rockets like other UFO's sighted through the ages, were seen no more in that form. []

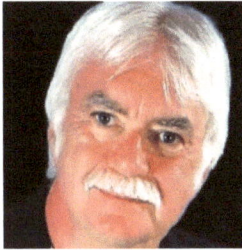

Hidden History

By
Rob McConnell

One has to wonder what the true facts are about history and how, if the truth were to be known, what effect it would have on this planet and it's humanoid inhabitants.

We know for a fact that Christopher Columbus did not discover the Americas that the Egyptians, Irish and Vikings were in the Americas both exploring and trading.

Egyptian artefacts have been discovered in the Grand Canyon and there have been recent archaeological finds that support a theory that the Chinese had made trips across the Pacific to North America before Columbus as well.

Archaeologists have found evidence that The Great Flood did really happen and as a result, the changes that were caused by the flood changed our planet and its inhabitants in many ways.

We know that prior to The Great Flood the oxygen level was twice as it is today.

Humans lived longer, were healthier and skeletal remains reveal that humans were taller, as were other living organisms.

This increase in planetary oxygen find was displayed at the World's Fair in Japan when scientists grew a tomato plant in an oxygen enriched environment.

The results could not be disputed. The tomato plant produced, and remember that we are talking about one tomato plant, 13,000 yes thirteen thousand tomatoes and the plant lived for more than six months.

The enriched oxygen would also validate the extremely long life of those spoken about in the pre-flood days in the Bible.

Trees have been found in the rich preservative peat bogs that have been measured to be over 1,000 feet!

Could the enriched oxygen atmosphere have a direct connection to the size of dinosaurs and other prehistoric plants and animals? According to archaeologist and international explored from New Zealand Dr Jonathan Gray, it most certainly does.

Archaeologists Round around the world know the truth and have for years and their discoveries and findings are blocked and suppressed by members of the scientific community as well as academia who egos and " mightier than thou" serves them well for funding and other personal gains.

I for one would like to know the truth despite the ramifications that the truth would have on history, the scientific community, academia or religion.

How can we expect the truth in from all members of society when we now know that the very historical basis of our existence and evolution on this planet and what our children are being taught in the hallowed halls of learning are lines.

We also know from archaeological finds that flight, batteries, electromagnet forces and mastered building skills were mastered by the ancients.

For more information on suppressed and hidden archaeology please Google Jonathan Gray and Michael Cremo.

David Nabham was on The 'X' Zone Radio Show this week and using present and historical lunar/tidal charts has developed an Earthquake Predictions System that would allow members of government and the media to let members of the public know of dates of high earthquake occurrences allow the public as well as officials the lead time necessary to prepare for the probable events for those dates.

As of yet there has been not been any interest from any government or official agency. There would be no cost whatsoever for this information which, if correct, and according to independent analysis of the data supplied by David Nabhan, it is, this information and data will save lives and the financial costs incurred by unexpected disasters.

For more information on David Nabhan or Jonathon Gray you can listen to their interviews on The 'X' Zone Radio Show at www.xzonepodcast.com.

Yes, the truth is indeed stranger than fiction.

Oh, and by the way, there has never been an archaeological find that proves the existence of extraterrestrial visitations.

For The 'X' Zone Radio/TV Show and The 'X' Chronicles Newspaper, I am Rob McConnell. []

Oped by Dan Perkins

An Army, is invading American!

By
Dan Perkins

The New York Times reported on Sunday July 5 that in the period of April 1st to June 30th 300,000 illegals entered the United States on the southwestern boarder. It is difficult for most Americans to comprehend 300,000 of anything, much less that many people in 90 days. I thought about it and I have come up with two ways to look at this number and a few ideas of how to stop it.

D Day had 150,000 troops.

Many people reading the article in the Times probably had no idea of D-Day and why it is important in world if not American history. I'm not sure this important historical fact is still taught in public schools. The Allies had to assemble the largest armada in the history of mankind to move 150,000 troops across English Channel to the French beaches in Normandy. Want another example?

How big is an Army infantry division?

According to the Department of Defense the typical size of an infantry division is 10,000 soldiers. The 250,000 adults that have entered into the United States in the last 90 days is equal to 25 divisions invading America and make no mistake they are coming to take control. It was estimated by the border patrol there be as many as 400,000 more are on the way.

The army has some new recruits.

We are now seeing, drug dealers, people from Asia, people from the Middle East just to name a few who are illegally crossing the border. There is no question that terrorists are using the on slot of illegal activity at the southern border to gain entrance to the United States. If the terrorists can find a weakness then they will exploit it to their advantage.

Some of the recruits can't be seen.

We have no medical history so we have to wait

until somebody gets sick to see what germs are being brought to us. World Net daily in an article on June 17th said," Carried by this tsunami of illegals are the invisible "travelers" our politicians don't like to mention: diseases the U.S. had controlled or virtually eradicated: tuberculosis (TB), Chagas disease, dengue fever, hepatitis, malaria, measles, plus more." This army attacks the young, the vulnerable and the elderly. When they get sick and die they are just as dead as if they were shot by a soldier's rifle.

How do we stop the invasion?

First, we notify the governments of the countries the immigrants came from:

We should redeploy the returning troops from Iraq and Afghanistan to the southwest border with order to repel all person trying to cross the border illegally. Upon placement of the troops they will immediately start deploying concertina wire in multiple layers. Next the Corp of Engineers will start to build walls of sufficient height as to prevent infiltration. Guard towers, close circuit cameras will monitor the walls and armed drones will work as observers and deterrents for illegals trying to cross. Neutral zones will be established well in advance of the border and warning signs in many languages and images will be posted and warning shots will be fired to individuals breaching the zone.

America currently has no enforceable border with Mexico. In 90 days 25 divisions of illegals have crossed our border, they have invaded our country. Our country is being attacked and our country estimates another 40 divisions are on the way. We are a sovereign nation, and we like any other sovereign nation has the right to establish and protect its borders.

It is time for America to enforce its borders to protect its legal citizens.

About Dan Perkins

Author and master storyteller Dan Perkins presents the first book in his trilogy about terrorism against the United States. The first in the series, The Brotherhood of the Red Nile, A Terrorist Perspective, has propelled him to national acclaim with interviews on radio, television and in-print. With the second installment, The Brotherhood of the Red Nile, America Rebuilds, we get a closer look into the mind of an ingenious writer. Picking up where book one ends, book two delivers more intrigue and mystery while striking terror in the hearts of readers as we ask the question: How in the world can we stop this from happening? Dan is a Registered investment adviser with 40 years of experience and splits his time between New Jersey and Florida.

Visit Dan Perkins on line at www. danperkinsatsanibel.com

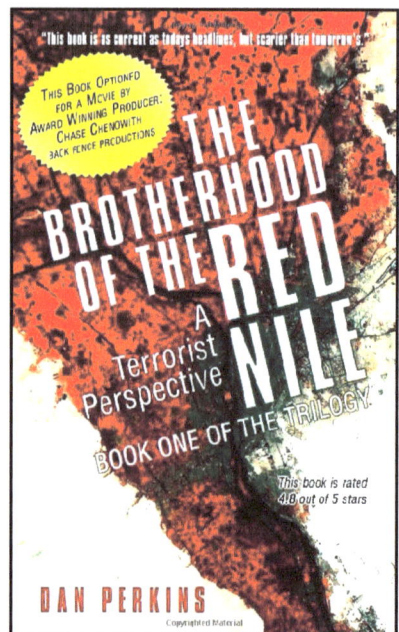

The Shroud of Secrecy Lifted on the St. Catharines, Ontario, Poltergeist of 1970.

5 Police Officers, 2 Priests, and a host of others witness a Poltergeist!

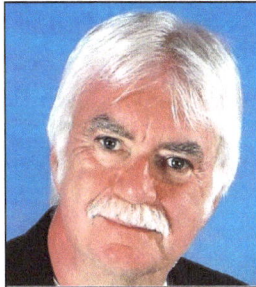

by Rob McConnell

According to retired Niagara Regional Police Officer Bob Crawford, when he responded to a domestic dispute at 237 Church Street, Apartment 1, in St. Catharines, Ontario, Canada's "Garden City" on February 6, 1970, the last thing that was on his mind was a poltergeist.

The poltergeist was carried by the media within the Niagara Peninsula, as well as national and international media, including CBC, CTV, CHML, The St. Catharines Standard, The Canadian Press, The Hamilton Spectator, The Toronto Telegram, The Toronto Daily News, and the Buffalo Evening News, just to name a few.

On Monday, October 2, 1995, in a home in St. Catharines, I interviewed Mr. Bob Crawford, Mr. Bill Weir and Mr. Mike McMenanin ,all retired members of the Niagara Regional Police Force stationed in St. Catharines.

Mr. Crawford recalled how on February 6, 1970, as he was leaving 237 Church Street, Apartment 1 where he had been dispatched to investigate a domestic dispute, a female who identified herself as a resident from another apartment in the building asked the officer for his help in their apartment.

Crawford followed the citizen into their apartment which was in total disarray.

The complainant told the officer their story of how objects and furniture were moving around their apartment by unseen forces. Crawford was shown a chest of drawers laying on its side in the kitchen. Crawford was told that objects and furniture started moving around on their own in their small church street apartment about 10 days prior to February 6, 1970.

Living in the apartment with the female complainant were her husband and two sons.

After listening to the complainant and the events surrounding the present state of the apartment, Mr. Crawford claimed that his first thought was to call a member of the clergy, when a priest from a local Roman Catholic Church arrived at the apartment. Crawford

stated that the priest was well aware of the events within the Church Street apartment and had been there previously and witnessed a bed moving away from a wall on its own. The priest then pushed the bed back to the wall but when he turned his head, again the bed moved away from the wall by unseen forces.

Crawford requested that everyone try to remain calm and instructed them to go into the living room.

Since Crawford was the last person to leave the kitchen, he claimed to have moved a chair out of his way and placed the chair in a normal position against the kitchen table before entering the living room.

While trying to calm down the complainant both Crawford and the priest head the sound of footsteps moving across the living room and into the kitchen.

Crawford claimed that he and the priest went into the kitchen and stated that the chair that he had moved against the kitchen table was in the middle of the kitchen several feet away from the kitchen table.

The priest told Crawford that this was the type of occurrence that had been happening for the past 10 days.

It was about this time that Constables Weir arrived. Constable Bill Weir who thought he was backing up Crawford on a domestic call was in for a "rude awakening."

After being briefed by Crawford, Weir, who was the officer assigned to this incident claimed that he had responded to this address earlier that year.

Weir said that he first responded to the address on January 15, 1970, and was made aware of strange occurrences which had been reported by the tenants of a different apartment. There had been reports of loud noises and strange occurrences. Since his first visit, Weir claimed to have contacted the Engineering Department of St. Catharines who inspected the building and found no structural damage with the apartment building.

The gas company was also called with the entire heating and water system inspected and everything was working fine and in good condition all well within normal operating specifications.

The police officers even bled the hot water radiators but still the noises persisted and so did the strange events of objects moving by unseen forces in Apartment 1.

Weir stated that while he was backing Crawford on the "domestic dispute" call on February 6, 1970, while in Apartment 1, he witnessed several bowling trophies being tossed off a wooden board over a radiator, being tossed off, one after the other, onto the floor. He also reported that he observed the kitchen wall clock unplug itself landing on the floor without making a sound.

The police officers who were at the scene that February 6 1970 evening claim that the "agent" or "host" of the described poltergeist activity was the 11-year-old son of the complainant. Crawford stated that when the 11-year-old walked through the apartment, pictures on the wall, "swayed in the same manner as a dog wags its tail when it is happy to see its master."

The officers all state that the invisible force pushed the young boy against the wall on several occasions and they also claim that as the boy was sitting in a large and heavy chair. the chair flipped over on its own pinning the child to the floor. The chair was so heavy that it took two officers to lift the chair.

The officers also stated that a chesterfield, holding four people, levitated about eighteen inches off the floor. One of the ladies who was sitting on the chesterfield fainted when she realized that she was sitting on a levitating piece of furniture.

Weir claimed that the child was sitting on the knee of a police officer when an unseen entity tried to remove the child. It took the strength of two officers to keep the child on the knee where he sat.

The officers also witnessed the child's bed levitating from the bedroom floor and watched as the frightened child jumped off the bed. The bed slowly then returned to the floor.They turned their attention to the frightened child and when they turned back to where the bed was, the bed was about two feet off the ground being supported by two chairs.

(Continued On Page 17)

YOU CAN BEAT LUNG CANCER:
Using Alternative/Integrative Interventions

Can you overcome lung cancer without harsh chemicals, surgery and debilitation? Are alternative interventions effective? Why do conventional physicians not use them? Can you prevent cancer recurrences and live into old age without chronic diseases and prescribed medications? This book answers these and other questions.

This is one of the most comprehensive books available on alternative treatments for lung cancer. It explains the treatments used successfully by a health professional/cancer survivor of 36 years and by some of the leading medical and health practitioners currently in the field. G. Edward Griffin, Author of World Without Cancer, The Politics of Cancer Therapy, and other books and films. Recipient of the Telly Award for Excellence in Television Production. President of American Media.

ABOUT THE AUTHOR: Dr Carl O Helvie (1932-) grew up in Gouverneur, New York and functioned as a nurse practitioner, educator, author, and researcher for 60 years. Most of his degrees and practice have been in public health and wellness. During his years in academia he wrote 10 books and book chapters, over 55 articles, gave 57 research papers around the United States and Europe, developed a nursing theory, and received funding for and established a nursing center and provided primary care for homeless and low income individuals and families. He also overcome lung cancer using natural interventions after being given 6 months to live by conventional medicine in 1974. Since retirement he has written two additional books and has been host of the holistic health radio show for the past 4 years. All of his current work since retirement from academia focuses on natural interventions for health problems. Applying these concepts in his own life he is now age 80 and free of chronic illnesses and prescribed medications dispite the average for a 75 year old of 3 chronic illnesses and 5 prescribed medications. In 1999 he received the Distinquised Career Award in Public Health from the American Publc Health Association, and most recently was listed in Wikipedia.

w w w . b e a t l u n g c a n c e r . n e t

The Shroud of Secrecy Lifted on the St. Catharines, Ontario, Poltergeist of 1970.

Continued From Page 15

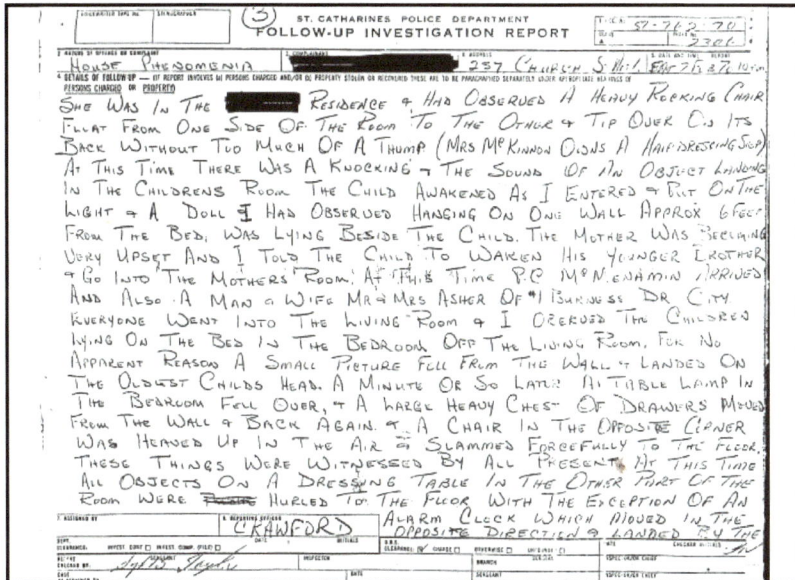

Dolls and pictures fell from the walls.

A table lamp in the bedroom fell over.

A large heavy chest of drawers moved away from the wall and back again.

A chair in the opposite corner of the room rose into the air and slammed down onto the floor.

The only two items that remained in the apartment which were not affected by the unseen forces of the poltergeist were a crucifix and a picture of the Virgin Mary with a palm leaf over the frame.

The police officers requested that the child's father make arrangements for the children to spend the night elsewhere. As the children started getting dressed to leave the apartment, a bookcase fell over.

According to one report, on February 11, 1970, police officers and detectives, including a police photographer with a 35mm camera, movie camera and tape recorder entered Apartment 1, 237 Church Street. Along with the police were two doctors, a lawyer, family members, members of the clergy, and the 11-year-old boy.

The police officers that their had been a leak and members of the media had been alerted turning the immediate area of 237 Church Street into a media circus. According to the officers, the family members could not leave their apartment building without reporters "badgering" them.

It was reported that a reporter for the National Enquirer tried disguising herself as a Nun hoping to get access to the family and the 11-year-old boy. The members of the family and the building owner hired a local lawyer who acted as liaison between the family and the media. The instructions from the family - NO INTERVIEWS.

Weir recalled that he personally advised the reporters that if they did not "back off" that they would be arrested and charged.

According to Weir, Crawford and McMenanin, the poltergeist activity stopped at the apartment when the 11-year-old boy left it and went to his grandmothers - or did it? There were unsubstantiated reports that the poltergeist activity continued at his grandmothers.

During the course of the investigation into this case, it was discovered that the "agent" or "host" of the poltergeist is now a successful business professional. I did contact the "agent" or "host" but he declined to be interviewed.

I understand and appreciate that paranormal experiences can be very traumatic, and that different people react in different ways. In the majority of cases, the "host" or "agent" have no recall of the poltergeist events. Others simply do not wish to remember, burying the memories deep within their conscious and sub consciousness.

I respected his wishes not to be interviewed and have therefore left the identity of the family out of this article.

I was able to contact one of the members of the clergy in this case, Father Stevens who was in Welland, Ontario, and he too, declined to my interview.

Based on the information given by the three distinguished members of the Niagara Regional Police Force that I interviewed, Bob Crawford, Bill Weir and Mike McMenanin, who have a combined total of more than 75 years police experience, that it this a very rare case of a highly documented poltergeist.

Paranormal researchers say, a poltergeist is usually associated with a spirit, usually mischievous and sometimes malevolent, which manifests by making noises, moving objects, and assaulting people and animals.

"Poltergeist" comes from the German "poltern" (to knock) and "geist" (spirit).

Some cases of poltergeist are unexplained and may involve actual spirits.

In other cases the phenomena seems to be caused by subconscious psycho kinesis (PK) on the part of one individual.

Most common poltergeist phenomena are :
- rains of stones, dirt and other small objects;
- throwing and moving of objects, including large pieces of furniture;
- loud noises and shrieks, strange lights, apparitions and vile smells.

In this case, based on the evidence supplied by Crawford, Weir and McMenian, and the subsequent police reports from the Niagara Regional Police Force, there were no vile smells, no drastic temperature changes, no raining of small objects, no strange lights and no apparitions.

The research of William Roll, project director of the Physical Research Foundation in Durham, North Carolina, has supported the psychological dysfunction theory pertaining to poltergeist activity.

Beginning in the 1960s', Roll studied written reports of 116 poltergeist cases spanning four centuries and more than one hundred countries. Roll identified patterns of what he called "recurrent spontaneous psycho kinesis" (RPK) which are inexplicable, spontaneous effects. He found that the most common "agent"

was a child or teenager whose unwitting PK was a way of expressing hostility without fear of punishment. The individual was usually unaware of being the cause of the disturbances, but was secretly or openly pleased with their occurrence.

Other researchers have found that "agents" are often in poor mental or physical health and thus are vulnerable to stress. Patients with unresolved emotional tensions have been associated with houses where poltergeist activity took place.

In studying the personalities of "agents", psychologists have found anxiety reactions, conversion hysteria, phobias, mania, obsessions, dissociative reactions, and schizophrenia.

In some cases, psychotherapy eliminates the poltergeist phenomena.

The psychological dysfunction theory has been disputed by other researchers, including Gauld and Cornell, who said that the psychological tests used were invalid. Psychiatrist Dr Ian Stevenson has proposed that spirits of the dead may account for more poltergeist cases than realized. In studying a number of cases attributed to living "agents" and to spirits of the dead, Stevenson noted significant differences.

The phenomena in living "agent" cases was without purpose and often violent, while cases involving spirits of the dead featured intelligent communication, purposeful movement of objects, and little violence.

According to Bill Weir, the poltergeist of 237 Church Street, Apartment 1, in St. Catharines, Ontario lasted 28 days - one complete lunar cycle.

For The 'X' Zone Radio & TV Show and The 'X' Chronicles Newspaper, I am, Rob McConnell. []

18 The 'X' Zone Directory of Who's Who

See Who's Listed In The 'X' Zone Directory of Who's Who : 2014 Edition

The 'X' Zone Directory of Who's Who 2014 Edition — Rob McConnell

ABBA, Ben
ADDABBO, Nunzio
ALLEN, Lisa, MH
ANGLIN, Elizabeth
APLEGATE, Sheila
ASIKA-ENAHORO, Chidi
ATHEY, Sandi
BAHTI, Tani
BALTHASER, Dennis
BARNETT, Lisa
BARTZ, Carolyn
BARYZA-LY, Janine
BATTROS, Mitch
BECKER, Rochelle
BECKETT, Shelby
BELITZ, Friar Justin, OFM
BILLE, Matthew A
BIRDSONG, Maighread
BISHOP, Dr. Jo Anne, PHD, MPA.
BLACKBURN, Alison Carol
BLACKBURN, Dr. Meg Losey, PH.D BLAZE, Chrissie
BLOOM, Howard
BLUE, Sebastien
BRASCHLER, Von
BROWNLIE. Marion
CAMERON, Tilde
CAMP, Robert Lee
CAMPIONE, David
CAROLE, CC
CARROLL, Judy
CHAMPION, David
CHAPMAN, Jim
CLARK, Daniel
CLEAR, Constance
COOK, Richard
CORNET, Dr. Bruce PH.D.
CROWE, Ray
DAHNE, Jill
DANELEK, J (Jeffrey) Allen
DANIELS, Kooch
DAVENPORT, Marc
DE ANGELIA, Dr. Angela
DE LONG, Douglas
DENNIS, Darlene
DONER, Margaret

DRUFFEL, Ann
DUPREE, Heidi, RN, CTN
DURANTE, Georgina
ELDER, Paul
ELLEN, Virginia
ENGST, Dorothy Jeanne
ENO, Paul F.
FENSTER, Dr. Michael
FIRODA, Tina
FLOWERS, Doyle
FOSTER, Brent
FREEMAN, Pattie, CI. CHT
FREER, Neil
FREUH, Deborah
FRISCH, Linda
GINEX, Nicholas Paul
GLADSTONE, William
GOLDYLOCKS TEMPLE OF HEALING
GRANT, Lois M, PH.D.
GREEN, Louisa Oakley
GREENE, Tara
GRUDER, Dr. David PH.D, DCEP
HADADY, Letha D.AC
HARMAN, Jeff
HARPER, John Jay
HAUCK, Dennis William
HAYNES, Dana
HELVIE, Dr. Carl 0
HICKMAN, Jim
HICKOK, Nita
HOGUE, John
HURIASH, Professor Solomon
JACKSON, Joyce
JACOBS, Linda
JAFFER, Hassan
JETT, Blair
JETTE, Martha
JOHANSSON, Linnea
JOHNSON, Kat
JONES, Carolyn CJ
JONES-HUNT, Jackie
JOSEPH, Mike M
JOYCE, Elizabeth
KARST, Patrice
KAYA
KIRK, Gayle
KITEI, Dr. Lynne MD
KNIGHT, Sirona
KOLB, Dr. Susan E MD
LARSON, Cynthia Sue
LASZLO, Dr. Ervin
LEMIRE, Dr. Luc
LEVIN, Deborah
LIEBERMAN, Ellena Lynn
LOUISE, Dr. Rita
LOVELAND, Dr. Bara H
MacLEOD-LUTCHIN, Dr. Nance PH.D/NMD/DNM
MANN, Lucia
MARDEN, Kathleen
MARINELLI, Gianni
MARRA, Dr. Joseph
MASSENGALE, Dr. Dee
McCONNELL, Rob
McDONALD, Lori Marie
McDONALD, William Louis, Sr.
McDONNOUGH, Michael
McKEEVER, Gracie E
MERCADO, Elaine, RN
MISS Bonnie
MONAGHAN, Kelly Joe

MOORE, Tom T.
MORGAN, Robert W
MYERS, Steven
NASH, Sarah
NOSEWORTHY, Olive Neil
NUNLEY, Ann P
OESTE, Sr. Dave, D.D.
OGDEN, Frank
OZOSKY, Edward
PALMERO, Joseph
PAYTON, Michelle A
PENTTILA, Nancy
PHENIX & PHENIX LITERARY PUBLICISTS
PRESCOTT, Heidi
PRICE, David
PSYCHIC Universe
PYE, Lloyd
RADJA, Shelley
RANDLE, Dr. Kevin
RAY, Rev. Peggy
RESS, Patricia Griffin
ROBINS, Barbara
ROGERS VAN COOPS, Dr. Margaret
SALAZ, Lisa
SCHENK, Nolalee
SCHNEID, Dr. William PH.D.
SENATE, Richard L.
SHANNON, Marilyn
SHAPIRO, Gerri
SHIMMER, John C
SIMS, Derrel
SOMAN, Rita
SPENCER, Gabrielle
STEIN, Matthew
STONE, Michael
SYSKA, Carol
TAFFS, Mary
TEAL, Michael Lucien
TRUE PSYCHICS NETWORK
TURI, Dr. Louis
UNDERWOOD, Mark
VIOLINI, Juanita Rose
WAGMAN, Freda
WAGNER, Angelica
WEGMAN, Dita
WEIL, Nancy
WILLARD, Billy
ZGOURIDES, Dr. George MD, PSYD

Get Listed In The 'X' Zone Directory of Who's Who In Print In eFormat and The Web at www.xzonedirectory.com

Register Online At www.xzonedirectory.com/register.htm

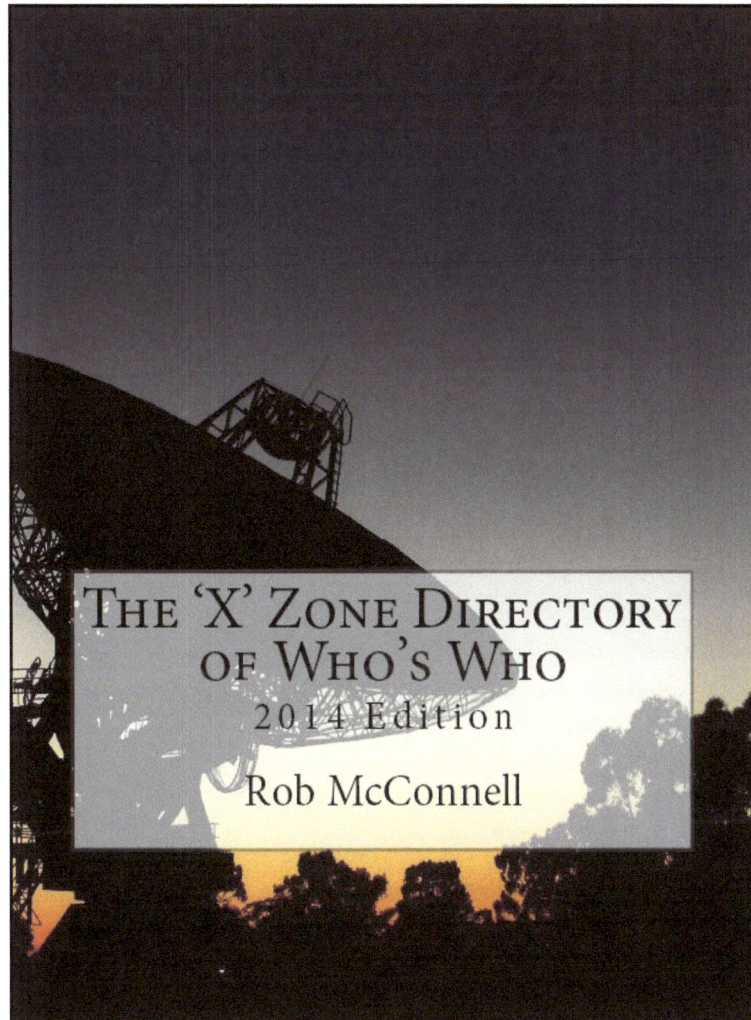

The Flying Dutchman and Other Phantom Ships

The sea has always held a fascination for human kind. It is vast, ruthless and unpredictable and some of the wonders of its depths have proved impenetrable even to modern science. Through the ages, the oceans have been a rich source of myth, legend, and superstition, as well as the scene of real mysteries and unsolved enigmas.

Stories of ghostly apparitions at sea are common. Perhaps it is not surprising that sailors on watch for hours over the immense wastes of the ocean should let their eyes deceive them. But tales of ghost ships and marine phantoms are no so easily explained away.

On the morning of July 10, 1918, toward the conclusion of the First World War, the U.S. submarine L-2 was patrolling at periscope depth off Cape Clear, Ireland, in the eastern Atlantic. Suddenly, her captain, Lt. Paul F Foster, sighted a target - the lean black shape of a German U-boat lying dead in the water. Clearly marked on the conning tower was the number 65, and to his surprise, he also saw the figure of an officer, arms folded across his chest, standing on the bow.

The U.S. submarine began to maneuver into attack position, but its torpedoes were not needed. A massive explosion erupted on the UB-65 blowing it into fragments. The whole incident had happened so quickly that the watcher aboard the L-2 could hardly believe what they had seen, particularly as they found no wreckage and no survivors. But on July 31, 1918, a terse bulletin issued by German Navel Headquarters confirmed that UB-65 and its 34-member crew was missing, presumed lost.

And that was the end or rather the beginning, of one of the most curious mysteries of modern naval history. For the submarine UB-65 seems to have been haunted during the whole of its brief two-year career.

Built at Bruges, Belgium, in the autumn of 1926, it was one of a batch of 24 U-boats destined for the Flanders Flotilla, and carried a crew of 3 officers and 31 men. It seemed jinxed from the start. Five men were killed during its construction, and just before the first test dive one man deliberately threw himself overboard. The dive itself was a disaster as the submarine was stuck on the seabed for 12 hours. Back in Bruges, while it was loading supplies for its first operational voyage, a torpedo exploded, killing 5 enlisted men and a 2nd lieutenant. It was this dead officer who was said to come back aboard the submarine, to walk the narrow confines of the crew quarters and to stand, arms crossed, on the bow.

"We were never a pack of nervous fools," wrote one of the submarine's petty officers, "...we saw the ghost; we never imagined anything. What we saw, we saw, and that was all."

Exorcism ordered

Admiral Gustav N. von Schroeder, the commanding officer at Bruges, ordered that the vessel be exorcised, but the hauntings continued. The leading gunner, named Eberhardt, committed suicide after seeing the phantom; Petty Officer Richard Meyer followed suit by jumping overboard and swimming out to sea. Finally, when the submarine's commander insisted to Schroeder that he too had seen the ghost, the entire crew was replaced. Just two weeks later, the U.S.S.S L-2 watched the submarine's mysterious, violent end.

A German naval psychologist Professor Hecht, conducted a thorough investigation into the haunting His report was never published, but he admitted that he could "put forward no alternative theory to the supernatural agency which finally brought about the destruction of this ill-fated vessel."

The Flying Dutchman

At least the UB-65 was a real ship. No one knows for sure whether the phantom vessel known as the Flying Dutchman has ever had any material existence. But it has been sighted, and its appearances have been recorded, in all the oceans of the world - on one occasion by a whole squadron of the British Royal Navy.

On July 11, 1881, H.M.S. Inconstant, sailing as part of Admiral Lord Clanwilliam's Detached Squadron, apparently encountered the phantom ship in the South Atlantic. On board the Insonstant were Prince Albert Victor, duke of Clarence, and his brother, Prince George, later King George V of England. Their account reads as follows: "At 4:00 a.m. the Flying Dutchman crossed our bows. A strange red light as part of the phantom ship all aglow, in the midst of which light the masts, spars, and sails of a brig 200 yards distant stood out in relief as she came up on the port bow."

Suddenly it was gone. Thirteen officers and men including the commander, saw the fiery ship, and it was sighted simultaneously by the crews of the corvettes Tourmaline and Cleopatra. As the legend of the Flying Dutchman predicts, the sailor who first saw the strange vessel fell to his death from the rigging that very morning.

An equally well-documented and more terrifying sighting occurred on the last day of February 1857, off Tristan da Cunha in the South Atlantic, when the Flying Dutchman swept across the bows of the cargo ship Joseph Somers. The crew and passengers later gave sworn depositions that they had seen the phantom ship's captain himself, a demonic Dutchman, with "dirty white curls streaming, moon-face a mask of malevolence..." As the ghost vanished, the ship's cargo burst into flames. Those on board were rescued at the last minute by the sailing ship Nimrod.

On May 13, 1866, the American sailing ship General Grant was wrecked in a vast cavern beneath the cliff of the Disappointment Islands in the Pacific. This area has been renowned for sightings of ghost ships for at least 300 years. The story goes that the General Grant had been pursued for days by a mystery ship that many aboard thought was the Flying Dutchman.

The mystery did not end there. The General Grant had been carrying a million dollars' worth of gold dust when it sank. Several salvage attempts were made, all unsuccessful. In March 1870, a salvage party of five men fro the schooner Daphane entered the cavern...and they were never seen again. Safely back on dry land, the remaining crew of the Daphane later reported that, as they lay at anchor, the Flying Dutchman had crossed their bows and disappeared into a ghostly haze.

Many other sightings have been recorded. The Flying Dutchman was seen twice in Galveston Bay, Texas, in 1892. On the second occasion, the Norwegian ship Fair Hilda almost ran aground while desperately trying to avoid it.

(Continued on Page 21)

The Flying Dutchman
and
Other Phantom Ships
Continued From Page 20

The Flying Dutchman is not the only ghostly vessel seen on the world's oceans. All down the coast of New England sightings of phantom ships are still to this day very common. One, regular enough to be a tourist attraction, appears between Christmas and New Year off the coast of Rhode Island in a red ball of fire, similar to that described in the Inconstant incident. Known as the Palatine Light, this is alleged to be the ghost of the 18th century Palatine, an immigrant ship deliberately lured ashore by wreckers. Various natural explanations for the appearance of phantom ships have been put forward. On the Caribbean Island of Carriacou, for example, where sightings of a ghostly white schooner are frequently reported, local point out a peculiarity of the Leeward Rocks. Approached from one point, they are simple needles of coral; from another they appear as eerily blanched sailing ships, driving toward the shore.

To those who claim to have seen it, the Flying Dutchman is real enough. Toward the end of the second world war, Admiral Karl Dienitz, Hitler's commander in chief of submarines reported: "Certain of my U-boat crews claim they saw the Flying Dutchman or some other phantom ship on their tours of duty east of Suez. When they return to their base the men said they preferred facing the combined strength of Allied warships in the North Atlantic rather than know the terror a second time of being confronted by a phantom vessel."

TOP 10 GHOST SHIPS

10. The Caleuche
One of the most well known legends of the Chilota mythology of southern Chile describes the Caleuche, a ghost ship that appears every night near the island of Chiloe. According to local legend, the ship is a kind of conscious being that sails the waters around the area, carrying with it the spirits of all the people who have drowned at sea. When spotted, the Caleuche is said to be strikingly beautiful and bright, and is always accompanied by the sounds of party music and people laughing. After appearing for a few moments, the ship is then said to disappear or submerge itself under the water. According to Chilota mythology, the spirits of the drowned are summoned to the ship by the Sirena Chilota, the Pincoya, and the Picoy, three Chilota "water spirits" who resemble mermaids. Once aboard the phantom ship, the drowned are said to be able to resume their life as it was before they died.

09. The SS Valencia
The SS Valencia was steamer ship that sank off the coast of Vancouver, British Columbia in 1906. The ship had encountered bad weather near Cape Mendocino, and after drifting off course, struck a reef and began taking on water. The crew quickly began lowering lifeboats holding the ship's 108 passengers into the water, but several of these

capsized, and one simply disappeared. The Valencia eventually sank, and only 37 of the roughly 180 people on board survived. Five months later, a fisherman claimed he had found a life raft with 8 skeletons in it in a nearby cave. A search was launched, but it found nothing. Thanks to its dramatic end, the Valencia eventually became the source of numerous ghost ship stories. Sailors would often claim they could see the specter of the steamer drifting near the reef in Pachena Point, and to this day the ship is the source of frequent wild theories and ghost ship sightings. In a bizarre twist, 27 years after the sinking of the Valencia, one of its life rafts was found floating peacefully in nearby Barkley Sound. The "ghost raft" was said to be in remarkable condition, and even still had most of its original coat of paint.

08. The Ourang Medan
The story of the Ourang Medan begins in 1947, when two American ships received a distress call while navigating the Strait of Malacca, off the coast of Malaysia. The caller identified himself as a member of the crew of the Ourang Medan, a Dutch vessel, and supposedly claimed that the ship's captain and crew were all dead or dying. The messages became jumbled and bizarre before trailing off and ending with the words: "I die." The ships quickly raced to the scene to help. When they arrived, they found that the Ourang Medan was undamaged, but that the entire crew—even the ship's dog— was dead, their bodies and faces locked in terrified poses and expressions, and many pointing at something that was not there. Before the rescuers could investigate further, the ship mysteriously caught on fire, and they had to evacuate. Soon after, the Ourang Medan is said to have exploded and then sank. While the details and the overall veracity of the Ourang Medan story are still widely debated, there have been a number of theories proposed about what might have caused the death of the crew. The most popular of these is that the ship was illegally transporting nitroglycerin or some kind of illegal nerve agent, which was not properly secured and seeped out into the air. Others, meanwhile, have claimed the ship was a victim of a UFO attack or some other kind of paranormal event.

07. The Carroll A. Deering
Perhaps the most famous ghost ship of the Eastern Seaboard is the Carroll A. Deering, a schooner that ran aground near Cape Hatteras, North Carolina in 1921. The ship had just returned from a commercial voyage to deliver coal in South America, and had last been spotted just south of Hatteras by a lightship near Cape Lookout. It ran aground in the notorious Diamond Shoals, an area famous for causing shipwrecks, and sat there for several days before any help was able to reach it. When they did arrive, the Coast Guard found that the ship was completely abandoned. The navigation equipment and logbook were missing, as were the two lifeboats, but otherwise there were no signs of any kind of foul play.

A massive investigation by the U.S. government followed, which discovered that several other ships had disappeared under mysterious circumstances around the same time. Several theories were eventually put forth,

the most popular being that the ship fell victim to pirates or rumrunners. Others suggested that mutiny might have been the cause, as the Deering's first mate was known to bear some animosity toward its Captain, but no definitive proof has even been discovered. The mystery surrounding the ghost ship has encouraged wild speculation, and many have argued that paranormal activity might have been responsible, citing the ship's passage through the infamous Bermuda triangle as proof that some kind of otherworldly phenomena might be to blame.

06. The Baychimo
One of the most amazing cases of a real-life ghost ship concerns the Baychimo, a cargo steamer that was abandoned and left to drift the seas near Alaska for nearly forty years. The ship was owned by the Hudson Bay Company, and was launched in the early 1920s and used to trade pelts and furs with the Inuit in northern Canada. But in 1931, the Baychimo became trapped in pack ice near Alaska, and after many attempts to break it free, its crew were eventually airlifted out of the area to safety. After a heavy blizzard, the ship managed to break free of the ice, but it was badly damaged and was abandoned by the Hudson Bay Company, who assumed it would not last the winter.

Amazingly, the Baychimo managed to stay afloat, and for the next 38 years, it remained adrift in the waters off Alaska. The ship became something of a local legend, and was frequently sighted aimlessly floating near the frozen ice packs by Eskimos and other vessels. It was boarded several times, but weather conditions always made salvaging it nearly impossible. The Baychimo was last sighted in 1969, again frozen in the ice off of Alaska, but it has since disappeared. The ship is believed to have sunk in the intervening years, but recently a number of expeditions have been launched in search of now nearly 80-year-old ghost ship.

05. The Octavius
Although it is now considered more legend than anything, the story of the Octavius remains one of the most famous of all ghost ship stories. The tale dates back to 1775, when it is said that a whaling ship called the Herald stumbled across the Octavius floating aimlessly off the coast of Greenland. Crewmembers from the Herald boarded the Octavius, where they discovered the bodies of the crew and passengers all frozen solid by the arctic cold. Most notably, the crew found the ship's captain still sitting at his desk, midway through finishing a log entry from 1762, which meant the Octavius had been adrift for 13 years. According to the legend, it was eventually discovered that the captain had gambled on making a quick return to England from the Orient via the Northwest Passage, but that the ship had become trapped in the ice. If true, this would mean the Octavius had completed its passage to the Atlantic as a ghost ship, its crew and captain long dead from exposure to the elements.

(Continued On Page 24)

Have an idea for a story?

Here is your chance to get your short story, poem or timely news article published in a newspaper.

We are looking for writers and budding journalists who want to submit their stories for publication.
(Your submission must be original work and it must not have been published elsewhere)
Submit to: Prism Publishing
P.O. Box 429, Cobalt, ON P0J 1C0
Fax: (705) 679-1144
e-mail: thevoice@prismpublishing.ca

www.prismpublishing.ca

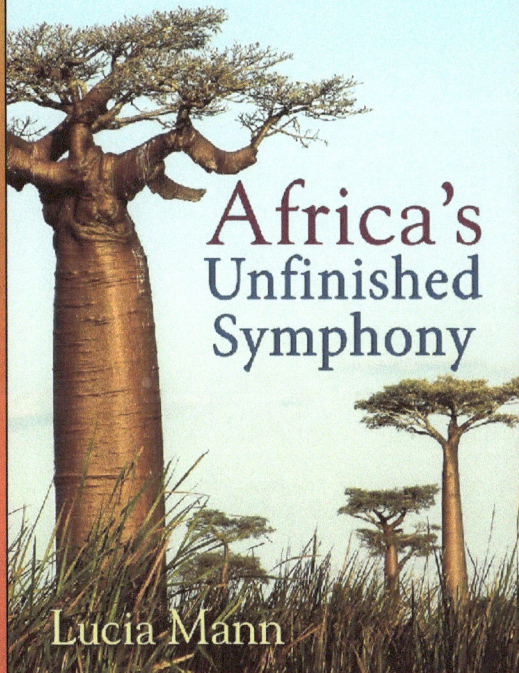

Top Ten
Ghost Ships
Continued From Page 21

04. The Joyita

The Joyita was a fishing and charter boat that was found abandoned in the South Pacific in 1955. The ship, along with its 25 passengers and crew, were en route to the Tokelau Islands when something happened, and it was not until hours later that the Joyita was reported overdue and a rescue attempt launched. A massive air search was undertaken, but it failed to find the missing ship, and it was not until five weeks later that a merchant ship stumbled upon the Joyita drifting some 600 miles off its original course. There was no sign of any of the passengers, crew, cargo, or life rafts, and the ship was damaged and listing quite badly to one side. Further inspection by authorities found that the ship's radio was tuned to the universal distress signal, and a search of the deck uncovered a doctor's bag and several bloody bandages. None of the crew or passengers was ever seen again, and the mystery of what happened has never been revealed. The most popular theory is that pirates killed the passengers and threw their bodies overboard, but other claims have included everything from mutiny and kidnapping to insurance fraud.

03. The Lady Lovibond

The UK has a long tradition of legends about ghost ships, and of these the Lady Lovibond is perhaps the most famous. As the story goes, the Lady Lovibond's captain, Simon Peel, had just gotten married, and decided to take his ship out on a cruise to celebrate. He brought his new bride along—going against a longstanding seafaring belief that bringing a woman on board a boat is bad luck—and set sail on Feb. 13, 1748. Unfortunately for Peel, his first mate was also in love with his new wife, and after watching the celebrations, the man became overwhelmed with rage and jealousy and intentionally steered the boat into the deadly Goodwind Sands, a sand bar notorious for causing ship wrecks.

The Lady Lovibond sank, killing all those aboard. As the legend goes, ever since the wreck the Lady Lovibond can be seen sailing the waters around Kent every 50 years. It was sighted in 1798 by a few different ship captains, as well as in 1848 and 1898, when it supposedly appeared to be so real that some boats, thinking it a vessel in distress, actually sent out life rafts to help it. The Lady Lovibond was again seen in 1948, and while there were no confirmed sightings on its most recent anniversary in 1998, it continues to be one of the most well-known ghost ship legends in Europe.

02. The Mary Celeste

Undoubtedly the most famous of all the real-life ghost ships, the Mary Celeste was a merchant ship that was found derelict and adrift in the Atlantic Ocean in 1872. The ship was in a seaworthy condition, with all its sails still up and a full store of food in its cargo hold, but its life boat, captain's log book and, more importantly, the entire crew, had mysteriously vanished. There was no sign of a struggle, and

the personal belongings of the crew and cargo of over 1500 barrels of alcohol were untouched, seemingly ruling out piracy as a possible explanation. In the years since its bizarre discovery, a number of theories have been proposed regarding the possible fate of the Mary Celeste's crew. These include that those aboard were killed by a waterspout, that the crew mutinied, or even that eating flour contaminated with fungus led all the passengers to hallucinate and go mad. The most probable theory remains that a storm or some kind of technical issue led the crew to prematurely abandon the ship in the lifeboat, and that they later died at sea. Still, the mystery surrounding the Mary Celeste has led to much wild speculation, and others have proposed everything from ghosts to sea monsters and alien abduction as possible explanations.

01. The Flying Dutchman

In maritime folklore, no ghost ship is more famous than the Flying Dutchman, which has inspired numerous paintings, horror stories, films, and even an opera. The ship was first mentioned in the late 1700s in George Barrington's seafaring book Voyage to Botany Bay, and since then its legend has continued to grow, thanks to numerous sightings of it by fisherman and sailors. As the story goes, the Flying Dutchman was a vessel out of Amsterdam that was captained by a man named Van der Decken. The ship was making its way toward the East Indies when it encountered dangerous weather near the Cape of Good Hope. Determined to make the crossing, Van der Decken supposedly went mad, murdered his first mate, and vowed that he would cross the Cape, "even if God would let me sail to Judgment Day!"

Despite his best efforts, the ship sank in the storm, and as the legend goes, Van der Decken and his ghost ship are now cursed to sail the oceans for all eternity. To this day, the Flying Dutchman continues to be one of the most-sighted of all ghost ships, and people from deep-sea fishermen to the Prince of Wales have all claimed to have spotted it making its never-ending voyage across the oceans. []

HISTORICALLY ATTESTED

* **1750 or 1760,** the SV Sea Bird: This merchant brig under the command of John Huxham (or Husham or Durham), grounded herself at Easton's Beach, Rhode Island. Her longboat was missing. She had been returning from a voyage to Honduras and was expected in Newport that day. The ship was apparently abandoned in sight of land (coffee was boiling on the galley stove) and drifted off course. The only living things found on the ship were a dog and a cat. A fictional account of how she became derelict appeared in the Wilmington, Delaware Sunday Morning Star for 11 October 1885.

* **15 May 1854,** HMS Resolute: This barque-rigged ship of the British Royal Navy, was abandoned after being beset by ice in Viscount Melville Sound, Canada. She had been one of four vessels from Edward Belcher's search expedition for John Franklin. The ship drifted some 1,200 miles (1,900 km) before it was found on 10 September 1855 off the coast

of Baffin Island, Canada, freed from the ice.

* **25 November 1872,** SV Mary Celeste: After passing Santa Maria Island in the Azores on 25 November 1872 (the last entry on the ship's slate), the SV Mary Celeste, a merchant brigantine became derelict in unknown circumstances. No boats were found on board. She was found on 4 December 1872 between mainland Portugal and the Azores archipelago. The ship was devoid of all crew, but largely intact and under sail, heading toward the Strait of Gibraltar. While Arthur Conan Doyle's story "J. Habakuk Jephson's Statement" based on this ship added some strange phenomena to the tale (such as that the tea found in the mess hall was still hot), the fact remained that the last slate entry was on the ninth day prior to the discovery of the ship.

* **29 August 1884,** the SV Resolven: This merchant brig, was found abandoned between Baccalieu Island and Catalina, Newfoundland and Labrador. Her boats were missing. Her logbook was posted to within six hours of being sighted. Other than a broken yard, she had suffered minimal damage. The galley fire was alight and the lamps were burning. A large iceberg was sighted nearby. It has been claimed that none of the seven crew members or four passengers were accustomed to northern waters and it was suggested that they panicked when the ship was damaged by ice, launched the lifeboat, and swamped, though no bodies were found. Three years later, Resolven was wrecked while returning to Newfoundland from Nova Scotia with a load of lumber.

* **1885,** The SV The Twenty One Friends: This three-masted (tern) schooner, was built in 1872. She was financed by a group of 21 Philadelphia Quakers and consequently named the Twenty One Friends. In 1885, returning to Philadelphia with a full load of lumber from Brunswick, Georgia, the ship was rammed by the John D. May off the coast of Cape Hatteras. Capt. Jeffries removed his crew and abandoned the vessel. The ship and cargo were left to the mercy of the sea. Capt. Jeffries' concern for the safety of his men was appropriate; however, the Gaskill-made ship proved herself to be more seaworthy than expected. After the collision, the ship was sighted on both sides of the Atlantic over the next two years. She finally came ashore in Ireland, where her cargo was salvaged and she was employed as a fishing vessel.

* **22 January 1906,** the SS Valencia's lifeboat no. 5: The lifeboat went adrift when the ship sank off the coast of Vancouver Island, British Columbia, Canada. The lifeboat was found floating in Barkley Sound, Vancouver Island, British Columbia, Canada in remarkably good condition 27 years after the sinking.

(Continued On Page 25)

Historically Attested
Ghost Ships
Continued From Page 24

* **October 1917,** the SV Zebrina: This sailing barge departed Falmouth, Cornwall, England, in October 1917 with a cargo of Swansea coal bound for Saint-Brieuc, France. Two days later she was discovered aground on Rozel Point, south of Cherbourg, France, without damage except for some disarrangement of her rigging, but with her crew missing.

* **January 1921,** the SV Carroll A. Deering: After passing Cape Lookout Lightship, North Carolina, U.S. on 28 January 1921, the Carroll A. Deering, a five-masted cargo schooner, became derelict in unknown circumstances. The ship's lifeboats and logbook were missing when she was found on 31 January 1921 at the Diamond Shoals, off the coast of Cape Hatteras, North Carolina. The final voyage of the ship has been the subject of much debate and controversy, and was investigated by six departments of the US government, largely because it was one of dozens of ships that sank or went missing within a relatively short period of time. While paranormal explanations have been advanced, the theories of mutiny or piracy are considered more likely.

* **3 October 1923,** the SV Governor Parr: This four masted schooner was abandoned by her crew after she lost her mizzen and spanker in a storm while sailing from Ingramport, Nova Scotia, Canada to Buenos Aires, Argentina. The damage incurred by Governor Parr was significant to the masts and deck of the ship; however, she did not sink. Several attempts were made to either destroy or tow this derelict to shore, but all failed. Governor Parr was sighted for many years after her abandonment as she covered large spans of the Atlantic Ocean. She remained a derelict and "menace to navigation," drifting as far as the Canary Islands. It is unknown what happened to her in the end.

* **24 November 1931,** the SS Baychimo: This cargo steamer was abandoned after being trapped in pack ice near Barrow, Alaska, U.S. and being thought doomed to sink. However, she remained afloat and was sighted at various times between 1931 and 1969 in the Chukchi Sea off the northwestern Alaskan coast without ever being salvaged.

* **3 October 1955,** the MV Joyita: After leaving Apia, Samoa on a refrigerated trading and fishing charter boat, the Joyita became derelict in unknown circumstances. The ship's dinghy and three Carley-liferafts were missing, and her logbook was also missing, when she was found on 10 November 1955, north of Vanua Levu, Fiji. A subsequent inquiry found the vessel was in a poor state of repair, but determined the fate of passengers and crew to be "inexplicable on the evidence submitted at the inquiry".

* **In 1959** an empty submarine was found in the Bay of Biscay off northern Spain. It subsequently became clear that she had been being towed by another vessel and that the chain had snapped.

* **1 July 1969,** the SV Teignmouth Electron: After the last entry in her log was made on 1 July 1969, the trimaran yacht became derelict in unknown circumstances. The vessel was found on 10 July 1969 in the North Atlantic, latitude 33 degrees 11 minutes North and longitude 40 degrees 26 minutes West. Investigation led to the conclusion that its sole crewmember, Donald Crowhurst, had suffered a psychiatric breakdown while competing in a solo around-the-world race and committed suicide by jumping overboard.

* **1975,** the SV Ocean Wave: Bas Jan Ader was lost at sea while attempting a single-handed west-east crossing of the Atlantic in a 13 ft pocket cruiser, a modified Guppy 13 named "Ocean Wave". The passage was part of an art performance titled "In Search of the Miraculous". Radio contact broke off three weeks into the voyage, and Ader was presumed lost at sea. The boat was found after 10 months, floating partially submerged 150 miles West-Southwest of the coast of Ireland. His body was never found. The boat, after being recovered by the Spanish fishing vessel that found it, was taken to Coruña. The boat was later stolen. Ader's mother wrote the poem From the deep waters of sleep after having what she described as a premonition of his death.

* **December 2002,** the MV High Aim 6: After the owner last spoke to the captain by radio when the ship was near the Marshall Islands, halfway between Papua New Guinea and Hawaii, on 13 December 2002, the MV High Aim 6, a longline fishing boat, became derelict in unknown circumstances. The Taiwanese police deemed a mutiny probable. The ship was found drifting with its crew missing on 3 January 2003 approximately 80 nautical miles (150 km; 92 mi) east of Rowley Shoals, Broome, Australia. The derelict was subsequently scuttled.

* **24 March 2006,** the MT Jian Seng: The tanker ship was found on 24 March 2006, drifting 180 km south-west of Weipa, Queensland, Australia. The ship's origin or owner could not be determined, and its engines had been inoperable for some time.

* **24 August 2006,** the SV Bel Amica: This classic schooner was found derelict near Punta Volpe, Sardinia, Italy on 24 August 2006. The owner later claimed to have gone home on 14 August 2006 to address an emergency. The Italian press suggested that he may have been avoiding taxation of luxury vessels. The Coast Guard crew that discovered the ship found half eaten Egyptian meals, French maps of North African seas, and a flag of Luxembourg on board.

* **18 April 2007,** the SV Kaz II: This 12-metre catamaran set sail in 15 April 2007. She was filmed passing George Point, Hinchinbrook Island, Queensland later that day and on that same day, late in the afternoon, the GPS data showed her to be adrift. She was found adrift on 18 April 2007 near the Great Barrier Reef, 88 nmi (163 km) off Townsville, Queensland, Australia. When boarded on 20 April, the engine was running, a laptop was running, the radio and GPS were working and a meal was set to eat, but the three-man crew were not on board. All the sails were up but one was badly shredded, while three life jackets and survival equipment, including an emergency beacon,

were found on board. A search for the crew was abandoned on 22 April as it was considered unlikely that anyone could have survived for that period of time. The coroner believed that the men may have fallen overboard.

* **28 October 2008,** the MV Tai Ching 21 (Chinese: 大慶21號): The last radio transmission from the Tai Ching 21, a fishing vessel, was made on 28 October 2008. The boat was found empty on 9 November 2008 near Kiribati. Its lifeboat and three life rafts were missing. The abandoned 50 ton Taiwanese vessel had been gutted by fire several days previously. No mayday call was received. A search of 21,000 square miles (54,000 square km) of the Pacific Ocean north of Fiji by a US Air Force C-130 Hercules and a New Zealand Air Force P-3 Orion found no trace of the Taiwanese captain (顏金港 Yán Jīn-gǎng) or crew (18 Chinese, 6 Indonesians, and 4 Filipinos).

* **January 2009,** the SV Lunatic: In December 2007 at age 70, Jure Šterk started a journey to sail around the world on his boat Lunatic. He used his amateur radio to communicate, and was last heard from on 1 January 2009. His sail boat Lunatic was spotted on 26 January, approximately 1,000 nmi (1,900 km) off the coast of Australia. The boat looked damaged and there was no sign of Jure Šterk on deck. Three months later, on 30 April 2009 the sail boat was found adrift by the crew of the science vessel RV Roger Revelle, 500 miles (800 km) south-eastern on position: Latitude 32-18.0S, Longitude 091-07.0E. The sails were torn and there was no one on board. After boarding they found that the last log entry was made on 2 January 2009.

* **March 2011,** the MV Ryou-Un Maru: This fishing vessel was washed away from its mooring in Aomori Prefecture, Japan as a result of a tsunami. The vessel was found adrift on 20 March 2012 about 150 nautical miles (280 km; 170 mi) off the coast of Haida Gwaii, British Columbia, Canada, floating towards Canada after nearly a year at sea, no crew believed to be on board. It was sunk on 5 April 2012 by the United States Coast Guard.

* **June 2012,** the T.T. Zion: This 31-foot, center console Jupiter boat landed on Fort Lauderdale Beach east of East Las Olas Boulevard around 1:15 a.m. on 20 June, with its navigation lights on and engines still running, according to the Sun Sentinel. The Sea Tow company that Fort Lauderdale authorities contracted to tow the boat said that the vessel appeared sea worthy and did not believe a mechanical problem had occurred. A wallet and cell phone belonging to the boat's owner Guma Aguiar were found on board, but no sign of him or any other passenger was found. Authorities on ATVs searched up and down the beach, but could not find sign of Aguiar. The Coast Guard commenced a search at sea. In August 2012, the Ft. Lauderdale Police Department said that even though the investigation remains open, there have been no significant leads in the case.

(Continued On Page

Historically Attested Ghost Ships
Continued From Page 25

Continued From Page 25

February 2013, the MV Lyubov Orlova: In January 2013, the Lyubov Orlova, a former Soviet cruise ship, was being towed to a scrapyard in the Caribbean when a cable snapped, setting her adrift in international waters, one day after leaving St John's, Newfoundland, Canada. On 4 February 2013 she was found approximately 250 nautical miles east of St John's (approximately 50 nautical miles outside Canada's territorial waters) and drifting in a northeasterly direction. The crew did not pursue the vessel due to safety concerns. Some news reports claimed it was adrift and populated with cannibal rats. In reality, it most likely sank in the Atlantic Ocean in international waters.

Ghost Ship Movies & Films

- **1935:** The Mystery of the Marie Celeste (a.k.a. The Phantom Ship) offers a fictional explanation for the events leading up to the discovery of the most famous of abandoned ships.
- **1943:** The Ghost Ship tells of mysterious deaths among the crew of the Altair, for which it is suspected the insane captain is responsible.
- **1952:** Ghost Ship is set aboard a yacht haunted by two murder victims (the previous owner's wife and her lover) whose bodies have been hidden under the floor.
- **1980:** Death Ship is about a lost Kriegsmarine prison ship haunted by the evil spirits of the dead crew. It now roams the seas for new victims, picking up survivors to abuse and kill after it sinks their ships.
- **2001:** The Triangle features a large abandoned cruise ship that is haunted.
- **2001:** Lost Voyage is a supernatural thriller about a group of people exploring the SS Corona Queen, which has emerged from the Bermuda Triangle after 30 years.
- **2002:** Ghost Ship is about the Antonia Graza, an Italian ocean liner lost at sea 40 years earlier, and now boarded by a salvage crew who soon encounter the ghostly apparitions of murdered passengers.
- **2003:** Pirates of the Caribbean: The Curse of the Black Pearl had the Black Pearl as a ghost ship. Its sequels Dead Man's Chest (2006) and At World's End (2007) feature another ghost ship Flying Dutchman.
- **2009:** Triangle is a psychological horror film about a group of friends on a yachting trip who discover the derelict ocean liner Aeolus. []

TILL THE END OF TIME

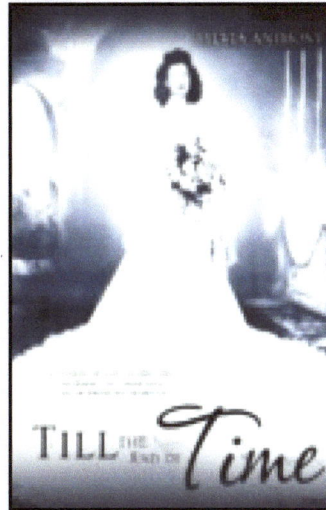

by Sylvia Anthony

Sylvia Anthony believes 'the golden years' are a time to gear up and get busy, not relax and take it easy. She has faced many hardships in her 84 years, but they seem to have made her stronger and more determined. As founder and president of Sylvia's Haven, a shelter for women and children near Boston, she has helped transform over 1084 lives in the past 27 years. While she hasn't been paid for the past four years, Sylvia wouldn't change it for the world and calls it her "magnificent obsession!"

Adding author to her vast repertoire, Sylvia's compelling biography, Till the End of Time (Xulon Press), is also being considered for a TV series! It is an extraordinary true story of abuse, love, sorrow and triumph that accurately portrays her rich emotional and personal journey from abused child to senior citizen.

Sylvia's story begins with her life as an unwanted child, beaten by her father and ignored by her mother, saved only by the love of God and her grandparents. Next come the teenage years and her first marriage that ended in divorce because of cruelty, but produced three children that she raised alone. And later, her second marriage to Rick that brought her closer to God and led to the founding of Sylvia's Haven, a shelter for the homeless.

After Rick's death, fate takes a hand in the next phase of Sylvia's life when a man she had cared for deeply as a teenager re-enters the picture to help her operate the Haven. Tony, her first real love, had unfortunately been convinced by his brother years before that he and Sylvia were far too young to go steady and they parted ways. Sadly, it was this decision that had pushed Sylvia into meeting her first husband who abused her.

Despite the fact that as a child she was made to believe she could do nothing right, Sylvia nonetheless went on to marry, raise three children by herself, and at 57 started Sylvia's Haven, a shelter for homeless women and children. Sylvia firmly believes that God not only gave her the courage to go on despite all the hardships, but keeps her healthy so she can open a shelter in all 50 states - and it's looking like it could very well become a reality with the recent application for additional property for a new shelter!

Sylvia's Haven is a nonprofit housing facility that provides shelter, guidance and emotional support for homeless women and their children. The women can be referred to schools, counselors and work advisers in the area for help with developing their own earning skills so they may live independent lives. Sylvia is also the author of Sylvia's Haven, published in 2008 by AuthorHouse. Please visit:www.sylviashaven.org for more information or to read testimonials from people whose lives were changed by Sylvia.

Sylvia Anthony has been featured on The 700 Club, and received a commendation from President George Bush in 2002. She is the recipient of the Arthur L. Whitaker Award, the National Alliance to End Homelessness Recognition Award, Ambassador for Peace Award, the Governor of Massachusetts Recognition Award, and was named the 2001 Hometown Hero by WBZ-TV in Boston.

www.sylviashaven.org

Lost Powers

In modern Western societies, most people consider those claiming to have psychic powers as oddities. But in ancient times, the early equivalents of today's mediums, channelers, or diviners were not viewed as freaks on the fringe of society.

From the Tingus and Inuits of the Arctic to the Jivaro of the Amazon basin, tribal peoples have traditionally depended on their shamans, or medicine men, to cure them of illness and to supply many other vital services, both practical and spiritual - from controlling weather conditions to communing with the spirit world.

The shaman, usually a male, may be chosen by heredity, succeeding his father in the role, or he may be marked at an early age by his unusual behaviour - having visions of spirits or gods, developing a taste for solitude, and wandering off alone into the forests or mountains for weeks on end, or becoming chronically absentminded and talking or singing to himself all day.

Chosen by the gods

But whether born to be a shaman or, as shamanic belief would have it, chosen by the spirits or gods, the would-be shaman generally must g through a dramatic crisis of initiation before he can adopt the role. In some cases, he may begin to see visions, working up to a climax in which he has convulsive fits and falls into a long period of unconsciousness. While the initiate is in this deathlike state, apparently induced by the power of suggestion, he experiences a horrific dream or vision. This ordeal prepares him for habitual contact with the spirit world. In some cases, he may witness his own death at the hands of evil. One shamanic initiate recorded that, in his vision, devils sliced off his head and then put it to one side so that he could watch while they dismembered the remainder of his body.

Changed perception

When the chosen young man recovers consciousness following his visionary ordeal, he will have the exceptional spiritual powers necessary to act as a shaman. In the 1930's one Inuit shaman told the Danish Artic explorer Knud Rasmussen what it was like to have attained that magical status: "I could see and hear in a totally different way. I had gained my enlightenment, the shaman's light of brain and body..." All the shaman's powers apparently depend on his ability to enter a state of trance in which, according to shamanic beliefs, his soul is separated from his body. The trance may be induced in a variety of ways. In some societies, the shaman fasts and mortifies his flesh in a hermit-like solitude until the necessary vision appears or spirit voices speak. More often, there is a public ritual with insistent drumming and rhythmic dancing. The suggestive power of the music and dance is sufficient to put the shaman into a trance state. In South America particularly, the shaman and other tribesmen may consume various hallucinogenic plants or

drinks.

When in a trance, some shamans experience possessions and speak with the voice of spirits - a practice very similar to that of spiritualist mediums. But most shamans simply provide a running commentary on what they witness and undergo during their psychic voyage.

Superhuman shaman

Shamans believe that, during a trance, their souls are separated from their bodies. This permits them to fly through the air at will, both across the earthly distances and through the supernatural spaces of heaven and hell. They can capture souls and steal or return them to their owners. They may communicate with spirits and with the souls of the dead. They may be capable of becoming invisible or disguising themselves as animals - usually the jaguar in South America. They can perceive events far off in time and space, and can kill an enemy from a distance. And they are impervious to both fire and pain.

There is no question that shamans, do experience visions and the illusion of flight. In 1961 anthropologist Michael J Harner, who was initiated into the shamanic practices of the Jivaro Indian tribe in the upper Amazon basin, reported his own dramatic experience during a trance in much the same terms as the Indians themselves:

"I found myself, although awake, in a world literally beyond my wildest dreams. I met bird-headed people, as well as dragon like creatures who explained that they were the true gods of the world. I enlisted the services of other spirit helpers in attempting to fly through the far reaches of the galaxy."

Bu the psychic flight does not always entail a vision of the spirit world. It may include a journey to another part of our own planet. Among the Jivaro Indians, shamans are frequently asked to see what a person is doing at a distant location - to check, for example, whether a woman is being faithful in the absence of her partner. Or the shaman may be asked to summon up the vision of a crime that has been committed, in order to identify the

perpetrators as effectively as a video camera monitoring the scene. Of course, it is extremely difficult to substantiate such claims, but in 1946 anthropologist Thomas Roessner produced intriguing evidence for the validity of shamanic visions. His claims were based on his experiences living among Indian tribesmen in the remote Ucayali River region of eastern Peru. The Indians, who had no contact with modern civilization, claimed to be in the habit of making spirit voyages to view distant cities. According to Roessner, "Indians have asked white men what those strange things that run so swiftly along the street: they had seen automobiles which, of course, they were not acquainted with."

Tribal responsibilities

The perceived practical value of the shaman to his tribe is manifold. He is responsible for controlling the weather, identifying the location of game, and interceding with the spirits to guarantee good hunting. He foretells the future and locates valuable objects that have been lost. His central function however, is to cure the sick. In the shamanic view of the world, illness is the result either of an evil object entering the body or of the soul of the patient being stolen. The shaman can embark on a psychic voyage to find the stolen soul and return it to its rightful owner, or he can suck the evil object out of the sick person's body.

(Continued On Page 30)

Secrets Of My Soul
by
Olive Neil Noseworthy

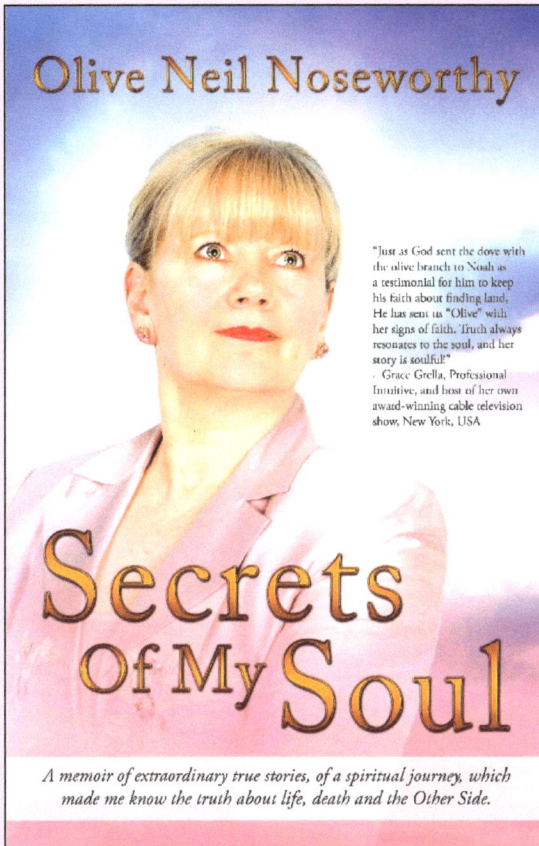

Olive Neil Noseworthy

"Just as God sent the dove with the olive branch to Noah as a testimonial for him to keep his faith about finding land, He has sent us "Olive" with her signs of faith. Truth always resonates to the soul, and her story is soulful."
- Grace Grella, Professional Intuitive, and host of her own award-winning cable television show, New York, USA

Secrets Of My Soul

A memoir of extraordinary true stories, of a spiritual journey, which made me know the truth about life, death and the Other Side.

Olive Neil Nosewothy is a Registered Nurse by profession with a Diploma in Mental Health and Psychiatric Nursing, a Bachelor Degree of Education, and a Master Degree of Educational Administration, obtained from Memorial University of Newfoundland and Labrador, Canada. She is currently pursuing a Doctoral Degree of Metaphysical Science.

She has travelled extensively throughout her life and has travelled to many faraway places, such as, The United Arab Emirates, Saudi Arabia, Europe, The Caribbean, South America, and North America. She has travelled to every province in Canada, as well as Canada's North West Territories.

Olive professes to be a psychic medium, who is blessed with spiritual gifts, including the gifts of clairvoyance, clairaudience, clairsentience, clairscent, intuition, telepathy, psychometry, remote viewing, healing, past-life regression, and the gift to make contact with loved ones who have died and who have crossed over to the Other Side. The other extraordinary gift she possesses to have is the rare ability to make contact with missing children and missing adults, and donates her time and special abilities to this great cause.

Olive is the founder and Executive Director of the Olive Angel Foundation, a non-profit organization, which is dedicated to help find missing children and missing adults. She is the founder and Executive Director of The Olive Branch, an organization established to promote peace and love throughout the world. And she is also the founder and Executive Director of Olive Seminars, and has given numerous presentations on spiritual topics such as, You As A Soul, A Past- Life, A Trip to The Other Side, Soul Signs, The Power of Prayer, The Other Side, Guardian Angels, and Guardian Souls.

Blessed with these extraordinary gifts, Olive devotes the remainder of her life here on Earth helping others know the truth; for she has been told that the time has come for the veil of secrecy to be lifted.

Olive is the author of, Secrets Of My Soul, a memoir of extraordinary true stories, of a spiritual journey, which made her know the truth about life, death and the Other Side, and she shares her innermost secrets and tells the world the answers to the mysteries of life. Her book, Secrets Of My Soul, can be purchased on her website: www.secretsofmysoul.org or from a bookstore or on-line at Amazon.com.

Her philosophy of life is similar to that of the fifteenth-century Jewish philosopher, Joseph Albo, whose belief is that we must not think that something is impossible, simply because our mind does not understand it.

As a Spiritual Health Consultant, she challenges you to explore, search, and seek the truth to greater empowerment and spiritual self-awareness. []

www.oliveneilnoseworthy.com

Lost Powers
Continued From Page 29

Paranormal powers

Some of the powers claimed by shamans are familiar to modern students of the paranormal. The experience of flight out of the body and of "seeing" places at a distance is generally equivalent to out-of-body experiences and clairvoyance. The shaman's healing practices are in many ways akin to those of Western faith healers, and the trance state of a shaman is so similar to that of some spiritualist mediums that anthropologists habitually refer to the trance-inducing tribal gatherings as "séances." There is a far higher proportion of shamans in tribal society than psychics in modern industrial societies. Among the Jivaro tribe, to take an extreme example, one in four males is a shaman. One possible explanation of this is that modern human beings have lost touch with the more irrational, instinctive, and spiritual side of their nature. Living in a scientific and rational world, they have perhaps suppressed their psychic abilities. Just as the human sense of small has declined in importance because people depend instead on their sense of sight, so psychic powers, if they exist, may have atrophied through lack of use, ignored by the rational self. If this view is correct, then prehistoric man living well before the age of science and reason, may well have been more in touch with the powers of the mind than we are today.

In the 1950's an Australian psychic researcher, Ronald Rose, set out to test this hypothesis by subjecting aborigines to rigorous ESP and PK experiments of the kind pioneered by Dr. J. B. Rhine at Duke University. Rose described the subjects of his test as semi civilized - in other words, they had abandoned their traditional way of life and largely adopted white Australian customs. But Rose felt that they were still close enough, in evolutionary terms, to their primitive ancestors to make the experiment worthwhile. The PK experiments turned out to be a total failure, with worse results than those usually obtained by the American college students often used by psychic researchers. But in the ESP experiments, performed with cards, 7 out of 12 aborigines recorded scores significantly better than chance.

In prehistoric times human beings were more in touch with their psychic powers than today. It is not surprising that a strong faith in such powers persisted in the early civilizations of Greece and Rome. In ancient Greece belief in the divinatory abilities of oracles was almost universal, shared by the common people and kings and potentates alike. Delphi was the site fo the most famous oracle, that of Apollo.

Prophetic trance

The Delphic oracle's prophecies were expressed through a priestess known as the Pythia, or pythoness, an uneducated woman who uttered the prophecies while in a trance. Her state of trance was probably induced by a series of ritual actions - sitting in the seat of the god Apollo, nibbling a laurel leaf, surrounded by the smoke of a powerful incense. Like a medium communicating with a spirit-being in a séance,

the Pythia took on a completely different voice when prophesying, as the god spoke through her. Although evidence from so ancient a time is hard to examine and assess, it seems clear that the priestesses who related the predictions of the oracles were what we would call "mediums" or "psychics." The often unintelligible utterances of the Pythia at Delphi were translated into verse by the priests of the oracle. The kings and emperors who sent to ask the oracle for information about the future often received a totally ambiguous answer, which they had t interpret as best they could. The practical uselessness of so many of the oracle's prophecies tends, of course, to encourage a skeptical view of the whole business. Btu much of what we know of the oracle at Delphi and other oracles is not inconsistent with what some researchers believe about psi. There were occasions, for example, when the oracle answered question before it was put, suggesting perhaps a telepathic reading of the inquirer's mind.

Many famous stories are reported from ancient times, especially of rulers attempting to test the psychic powers of the oracles. In about A.D. 100, the Roman emperor Trajan is said to have set a test for the oracle of Jupiter at Baalbek in Syria (now in the Lebanon.) This oracle was famous for its ability to read messages in a sealed container. To trick the oracle Trajan sent to Baalbek blank tablets of stone in a sealed box, asking for an answer to the questions written on them. The oracle sent back the box, with the seal unbroken, and an answer - a blank sheet of papyrus. []

The Thrill of a Lifetime
By William S Peckham

"Barb, this looks like a great hole for your nine iron," Sandra, her caddy, said.

"Really? I thought maybe I'd use my eight iron. Am I that far off?"

"You might over shoot the green. After all it's only a hundred and fifty yards."

Sandra handed Barb the nine iron. She had been Barb's caddy all through her golf days in Riverside High. Now, Barb, after graduating from Riverside with honours, was getting ready

for university–a BA in athletics. She had applied for an athletic scholarship, majoring in golf, and had been accepted at The University of Oak Mount. Barb had her sights set on a major in athletics.

"Now take your time, Kid. Remember it's only a game," Sandra said.

"Yeah, just a game. Like if I don't win I won't go to university, eh?"

"Don't worry. You've been accepted and the papers are all signed. Your acceptance doesn't depend upon this game... just your ego. Now, straight down the middle... easy does it. You're lined up perfectly. Just make that easy swing of yours count."

Sandra tried to sound calm, but she knew that Barb wanted to... no, needed to win this tournament, if she wanted go on to professional golf. Barb had told her that professional golf was not on her list of things to do in life, but knew that if she won this tournament she would qualify for the professional tour.

The official held up his hand calling for silence. You could hear the proverbial "pin drop". The back swing... slow... deliberate... just the way Barb had learned to do it. The swing forward... contact with the ball and the game hung in the balance as the ball soared towards the green.

All those tedious days of lessons, practice, driving and putting ranges were about to pay off. The eighteenth hole was short, as eighteenth holes go, but it was a killer for some golfers. The east-west fairway was straight as a draftsman's T square, lined with tall trees... a bunker on the left–fifty yards out, a bunker on the right, one hundred and twenty yards out and a huge bunker on the front left of the raised green.

Barbara and Sandra had walked this course several times before the tournament began and decided it was an easy par, providing Barb kept the ball straight... no hooks or slices. The wind could be a factor, if there were a wind, because it blew from the tee to the green, but the trees lining the fairway could turn it into a whirlwind.

The silence was so profound... you could hear it. Not a rustle of a leaf, not a bird chirping, not even a movement in the crowd. Mouths were open; heads swiveled to follow the flight... the ball started its decent to the green... on target... thud... roll and that hollow, clunk... the unmistakable sound of a golf ball going in the cup. A sound like no other you will ever hear. The crowd broke the silence with a roar, which could be heard across the nation.

"Barb... it's in the hole... a hole in one... Barb you did it," Sandra screamed and hugged Barb. "You're going to the LPGA.

"Yeah! Not bad for a blind golfer, eh."

ABOUT THE AUTHOR:

William Peckham's background in the DIY industry covers nearly fifty years. He is now in his mid eighties and the author of over one hundred and five short stories, two short story publications and has a mystery novel, "Out of the Woodwork". His non-fiction book, "Never Hang Wallpaper With Your Wife" was his first creation. His DIY columns have appeared in national newspapers. Visit www.williamspeckham.com []

The End of UFOlogy Is At Hand

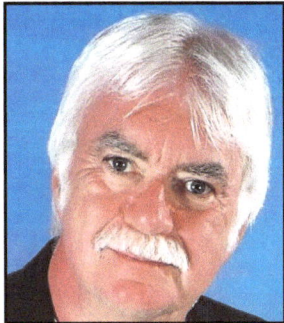

by
Rob McConnell

Members of the UFO community have been claiming, since the events of 1947 in Roswell, New Mexico, that the US Government and other governments of the world (yes, including Canada) have been suppressing information that would prove the existence of extraterrestrials and alien contact with certain members of government .

This week, the UFO community suffered a staggering blow to the claims of UFO Cover-up/Conspiracies, and I hope a well needed "wake-up" call when the The Disclosure Petition II - The Rockefeller Petition put forth by Stephen Bassett did not achieve the necessary signatures to require a response from the White House and was removed from "We the People" on March 25, 2012.

The Disclosure Petition II was posted on the White House website for sixty days (including the first submission on December 1, 2011) and drew minor media attention from accredited journalists, radio/TV, but mostly from internet bloggers and UFO enthusiasts.
The fact of the matter is that 25,000 signatures were needed to keep the petition alive.

Stephen Bassett, who was on The 'X' Zone Radio/TV Show, February 15 2012 said that the petition signing was not just limited to the citizens of the US but open to the world.

I quickly pointed out to Bassett that according to the US Census of July 2011, the population of the United States was 311,591,917 and a worldwide population count of 6,840,507,003 (2010) and that if the total number of 25,000 signatures were the magic number, and with all the people worldwide that UFO enthusiasts claim that there are, the number of 25,000 should be a very easy number to reach - if in fact the UFO phenomena was real - and not the claims of a few.

As I predicted, the Disclosure Petition II - The Rockefeller Initiative failed to get the necessary 25,000 votes with a worldwide final count of 6,937 (18,063 short.)
It is apparent that the people of the world have spoken out loud and clear that the UFO phenomena is a dying issue as evidenced by the sad showing of signatures on the Disclose Petition II.

Here are the facts:
- There are 311,591,917 people in the United States (US Census July 2011);

- There are 6,840,507,003 people worldwide (Including the US 0 2010);
- 25,000 signatures were need to keep the petition alive;
- 0nly 6,937 signatures were collected worldwide;
- therefore - 0.000001014106118 of the world population signed the Disclosure Petition II - The Rockefeller Initiative.

The excuses for the very poor response to the Disclosure Petition II - The Rockefeller Initiative and the removal of the petition from the Government website, "We the People" were quick to come from Stephen Bassett and the Paradigm Research Group:
- the 25,000 signature threshold, increased from 5,000.
- decrease in the public engagement of "We the People" after the threshold increase to 25,000. During the first sixty days after "We the People" was launched on September 22, 2011, between 15,000 and 20,000 petitions were submitted. During the past sixty days petition submissions were a small fraction of that number. The result has been far less traffic to the site and fewer crossover signatures. At this time only sixty petitions are active and many of those are early submissions waiting on a response.
- serious problems signing the petition. From early December forward PRG received many complaints from people having great difficulty signing the DP II
- petition fatigue. The "We the People" project is now five months old and many are a bit weary of being prompted to sign petitions.
- media coverage of the "We the People" project and submitted petitions has decreased substantially.

In an email to Bassett earlier this evening, I said, "It would seem that the world wide interest is based on the 'disinformation' being spread by the UFO community itself. In my opinion - it is not the government who is suppressing the information on UFOs but the UFO community who is claiming that the government is suppressing the information as a ploy not to have to provide evidence for their vague and un substantiated UFO claims."

Bassett has yet to reply.

In a move to try and keep the UFO / government conspiracy momentum going and to keep stirring the political pot, Bassett has not launched a new petition, Disclosure Petition III - Nuclear Weapons Tampering.

The new Disclosure Petition III - Nuclear Weapons Tampering - is calling attention to extraordinary claims and allegations from former ranking members of the United States Air Force. It is part of the White House's "We the People" project.

(Continued On Page 32)

The End of UFOlogy Is At Hand

Continued On From Page 31

On September 27, 2010 at the National Press Club in Washington, DC a press conference was held in which testimony regarding incidents of weapons tampering by unidentified craft was presented to the media. Those former members of the USAF who were present, making the extraordinary claims and allegations include self-proclaimed witnesses were all former U. S. Air Force personnel and included Lt. Col. Dwynne Arneson, Capt. Bruce Fenstermacher, Col. Charles Halt, Capt. Robert Jamison, Patrick McDonough, 1st Lt. Jerome Nelson, and Capt. Robert Salas. According to PRG's recent press release, most of these witnesses have held high security clearance.

This is the second time that these people have tried to get more than their 5 minutes of fame and glory, which again failed miserably.

Once again, let's look at the numbers and see why people are not taking these claims seriously:

- If there is or was nuclear tampering of the U.S. nuclear arsenal, why are there only a hand full of military personnel coming forth with these claims of UFOs tampering with the U.S. nuclear weapons?Once again, let continue looking at the fats... the numbers:

- 3,627,131 - the Total Number of "Active" Military personnel in 2009;

- 883,616 - The Total Number of "Reserve" Military personnel in 2009;

- 97,976 - Other DOD Personnel;

- 7 members or 0.000001535518068of the military claim UFOs were tampering with the US nuclear arsenal ;

- or - 4,558,722 or 99.999% of the military have not seen extraterrestrial craft tampering with the U.S. nuclear arsenal.

Another story that we broke on The 'X' Zone Radio/TV Show was when one of the most respected Roswell / UFO researchers and authors stated that new evidence has come forth which might prove that the Roswell, New Mexico event of 1947 was NOT a crashed UFO!

According to Dr Kevin Randle (Major in the National Guard Reserve), a group of Roswell UFO/Crash investigators, researchers and authors are taking a hard look at this new evidence and will be revealing their finding in the near future.

What will happen if after all these years and all of the claims that have been made by authors, researcher, investigators and even the new claims of government conspiracies and cover-ups when it comes to aliens and UFOs?

Undoubtedly, there will be a great number of people who will be back paddling and they will find a new reason why not to trust the word of these highly respected who are honest enough to come forth with their findings.

In my opinion, the end of UFOlogy is at hand. []

Personnel in Each Service					
As of May 2009 - Female numbers as of 30 September 2009					
Component	Military	Enlisted	Officer	Female	Civilian
Army	548,000	456,651	88,093	74,411	243,172
Marine Corps	203,095	182,147	20,639	12,290	34,000
Navy	332,000	276,276	51,093	51,029	182,845
Air Force	323,000	261,193	64,370	64,137	154,032
Coast Guard	41,000	32,647	8,051	4,965	7,396
Total Active	1,445,000	1,174,563	224,144	203,375	580,049
Army National Guard	358,391				
Army Reserve	205,000				
Marine Corps Forces Reserve	40,000				
Navy Reserve	67,000				
Air National Guard	107,000				
Air Force Reserve	67,000				
Coast Guard Reserve	11,000				
Total Reserve Components	833,616				
Other DOD Personnel					97,976

A Conspiracy Theory
The Reptilian Elite

They are among us. Blood-drinking, flesh-eating, shape-shifting extraterrestrial reptilian humanoids with only one objective in their cold-blooded little heads: to enslave the human race. They are our leaders, our corporate executives, our beloved Oscar-winning actors and Grammy-winning singers, and they're responsible for the Holocaust, the Oklahoma City bombings and the 9/11 attacks ... at least according to former BBC sports reporter David Icke, who became the poster human for the theory in 1998 after publishing his first book, The Biggest Secret, which contained interviews with two Brits who claimed members of the royal family are nothing more than reptiles with crowns. (Picture Dracula meets Swamp Thing).

The conspiracy theorist and New Age philosopher, who wore only turquoise for a time and insisted on being called Son of God-Head, says these "Annunaki" (the reptiles) have controlled humankind since ancient times; they count among their number Queen Elizabeth, George W. Bush, Henry Kissinger, Bill and Hillary Clinton and Bob Hope. Encroaching on other conspiracy theorists' territory, Icke even claims that the lizards are behind secret societies like the Freemasons and the Illuminati. Since earning the dubious title of "paranoid of the decade" in the late 1990s, Icke has written several books on the topic, including his latest work, The David Icke Guide to the Global Conspiracy, while operating his own website — complete with merchandise and advertisements.

Mr. President: If not America then who?
By Dan Perkins

I have been watching the news about what America is doing to help the Christians and Muslims stranded on Sinjar mountain in Northern Iraq. As I understand the president has ordered food and water to be dropped on the mountain. In addition the president has ordered selective air strikes upon military targets. The administration has not released the details as to the length of the humanitarian aid flights. Very little was released describing the type and number of ISSI targets other then to say they have destroyed some artillery and some convoys.

From what I was able to gather before we dropped the supplies Christians and Muslims were already burring their dead in shallow graves on the mountain who died for a lack of food and water. The Christians had to make a choice, stay on the mountain and die from starvation and dehydration or go down the mountain and face death for their faith. No doubt that some people in order to live have already renounce their religion.

My first question Mr. President where you waiting to see if some other nation would step in a feed and give water to those people on the mountain? It appears that the greater cooperation of nations you were looking for did not materialize in this crisis. When nobody stepped up to save those Christian and Muslin's you finally stepped in and helped save them, at least for now.

(Continued On Page 38)

Angels!

Are you curious about Angels?

My name is Alison Carol Blackburn

Since 1995 I have been working as an Angel Intuitive Counselor and Advocate. Using intuitive and psychic abilities I have been helping people to make and sustain their own Angelic and Divine Connections! This is done through private sessions and our regularly held Guided Angel Meditation Circles.

If you would like to know more about the Angels & to deepen your relationship with the Divine Realms, please visit our website:

angelicloveandlight.com

or call Carol at 514 631 5759

DID TIME TRAVELERS HELP THE ALLIES WIN WORLD WAR TWO?

Eddie Upnick interviewed Mr. Sidney Dowse in Antigua in 1995. Sidney worked on special assignment for Stewart Menzies (the head of MI-6) as the war broke out, and related top secret stories to Upnick under the condition that they would not be revealed until after Sidney Dowse's death, which occurred in 2008.

Stewart Menzies told Sidney Dowse this unbelievable story years after World War II ended. Stewert Menzies claimed to have met two men carrying hand-held, voice-activated devices in July of 1939, months before Germany invaded Poland. These men gave Menzies the code keys to break the German Enigma codes and improved the fledgling English radar systems. They also handed Menzies a piece of paper with 19 names on it, which was a list of German spies working in Britain. When Menzies asked them if they were German defectors, they responded; " No, we aren't German defectors, we are here to make sure a certain future doesn't happen."

Time Will Tell may read like pure fiction, but Upnick claims thirty top secret facts are hidden inside the walls of this "novel."

Dowse became much more famous for the fact that after the war started, his plane was shot down and he was captured and eventually sent to Sagan, the prison camp portrayed in the 1963 movie "The Great Escape". Sidney was a tunnel king who escaped along with 75 other men, 50 of whom were shot by the Gestapo.

Did Churchill know the date and time of the Pearl Harbor attack weeks beforehand?

Was Neville Chamberlain the fool history has portrayed him to be?

What was Joseph Kennedy's role?

Were ancient writings, dating back to 155 million years ago, discovered in North Dakota? What did they tell us?

Upnick also interviewed top level directors at Area 51 to look for second sources for Menzies stories.

These questions and hundreds more are answered in this amazing book. Fact or fiction, let the reader decide.

CREDENTIALS: Eddie Upnick was the inventor of Super Chess, a Games Magazine strategy game of the year in 1984. Upnick worked as a joke writer in the 1970's, working with Rodney Dangerfield among others. A situation comedy writer in the 70's and 80's, before beginning his detailed research for
- Time Will Tell,
- Future Tense
- 2052

www.EddieUpnick.com

Looking Into Death

"Through the study of the NDE (Near-Death Experience), psychology and science have shown that even the mysteries of death and the Great Beyond can be evaluated with scientific rigor." D. Scott Rogo, The Return from Silence.

In 1978, a 52-year-old night watchman suffered his second massive heart attack and his second near-death experience (NDE). Almost incredibly, he felt as if he had left the confines of his body and found himself looking down at his own heart operation. He later described in extraordinary detail what he saw the surgeons doing:

"They took some stitches inside me first before they did the outside...the heart doesn't look like I thought it did. It's big. And this is after the doctor had taken little pieces off it... [The surface was] pinkish and yellow. I thought the yellow part was fat tissue or something. Yucky, kind of. One general area to the right...I could draw you a picture of the saw and the thing they used to separate the ribs with. It was always there...It was draped all around, but you could see the metal part of it. I think all they used that for was to keep it constantly open."

The patient also claimed to have overheard the surgeons' technical discussion about what they were planning to do, which he was able to report in detail following the operation. But perhaps the most amazing details were his observations that one doctor had blood under one fingernail and that the other wore patent leather shoes!

Inexplicable observations

It was the details of NDE's such as this, where the patient correctly described the medical procedure used in his own operation, that persuaded Dr. Michael Sabom, of the University of Florida, that the phenomenon could not be explained away easily.

In 1976, prompted by the pioneering work of Dr. Raymond Moody, Dr, Sabom, together with their psychiatric social worker Sarah Kreutziger, decided to try to find people who had just NDE's among his own hospital patients. At the outset Dr. Sabom was by no means convinced of the authenticity of the NDE, and he expected to find a rational scientific explanation for the phenomenon. Sabom and Kreutziger did not have a long time to wait for their first near-deather, and their findings among early subjects were quite dramatic.

The third resuscitated patient they talked to reported a classic NDE, one that almost tallied with those reported by Dr. Moody.

Dr Sabom went on to study a large number of NDE's, including seven cases like that of the night watchman, where near-deathers correctly described surgical procedures. In one of these cases, a near-deather remembered the highly technical use of a defibrillator (a piece of equipment that sends a burst of electricity through the heart to control a rapid or uncoordinated heartbeat), Dr. Sabom wrote that this was "not something he could have observed unless he had actually seen the instrument in use."

Likely subjects

Within a couple of years, Dr. Sabom had collated his findings and felt confident enough to state that between 27 and 42 percent of resuscitated patients report an NDE. He also noted that patients who were unconscious for more than 60 seconds were more likely to have NDE's than those who were brought back to consciousness quickly.

Dr. Sabom confirmed that the stories recounted by people who had experienced an NDE were often astonishingly similar. While their consciousness was separated from their bodies, subjects regularly reported feeling detached from, and able to observe, their unconscious form. Many also stated that they had been taken on a mystical journey from which they were extremely reluctant to return.

Dr. Moody's own research, and that of all the subsequent workers in this new field, leads inescapably to the conclusion that there is a distinct pattern to the NDE, something that Dr. Kenneth Ring's study underlined. He concluded that the NDE unfolds in sequential stages, and the more deeply the patient enters the NDE, the more stages he or she experiences.

The dark side

In Britain, psychologist Dr. Margot Grey amassed evidence for the NDE that seemed to parallel the work of the American researcher. She became interested in the subject after having had her own NDE while touring India in 1976. Dr Grey took 18 months to assess the case histories of 41 subjects from Britain and the U.S.A. Much of her research replicated the idea of the "classic" NDE, where blissful sensations and heavenly figures give comfort. But there was a frightening difference. She also had discovered that a significant proportion of near-deathers reported "negative" experiences, something that cardiologist Dr. Michael Rawlings had found also.

These NDE's terrify patients and make them glad to return to life. Some patients, however, report a negative NDE followed by a blissful experience, which suggest a kind of instant purgatory. This aspect of NDE research is hotly contested. Some researchers, such as Dr. Sabom, deny the very existence of the negative experience, and it certainly takes some of the comfort out of the idea of NDE's. There seems to be no known rule that decides who has which type of experience, although Grey and Rawlings report that attempted suicides seem to suffer more negative NDE's. The study of the NDE only started in the 1970's, and it is becoming obvious that the published findings represent only the tip of the iceberg. Many thousands, arguably millions, of ordinary people may have had an NDE and kept quiet about it, being fearful of ridicule or because the experience was just too intimate to share with others.

A common encounter

The researchers are sensibly cautious about declaring any hard-and-fact conclusions at this stage in their studies, but some major finding have emerged. The NDE is certainly an experience shared by many normal people. If the NDE does not confirm the existence of another realm beyond death, it clearly does show that there are certain aspects of the human imagination and workings of the mind never previously anticipated. The experience appears not to depens on any religious background, but on some consistent reality. It does not rely on our knowledge of the experience, for as Dr. Sabom and Dr. Grey have shown, those who know about NDE's are less likely to have them, or at least less likely to remember and report them. It seems not even to rely on our individual wishful thinking or vivid imagination, for the experiences of prosaic adults and young children are very much the same.

(Continued On Page 37)

Who Is This Babylon?

by Don K. Preston, D.Div.

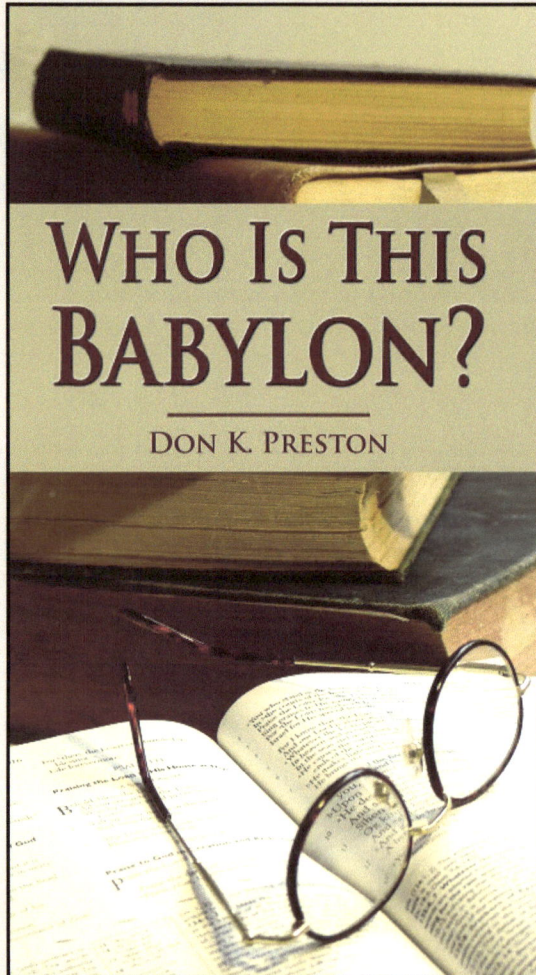

Looking Into Death
Continued From Page 35

The Core Near-Death Experience

When scientists began to look at their research material as a whole, they soon realized that the reports of NDE's followed a similar pattern in most cases. As a result, they were able to come up with an account of the basic "core experience":

- The subjects are dying, and gradually begin to feel blissful sensations.

- At the point of clinical death, they feel they are leaving their body (an out-of-body experience, of OBE) and floating above it, looking down with detachment or even amusement. They may observe incidents or overhear conversations that are verified late.

- They enter an area of darkness, commonly described as a long tunnel.

- Many near-deathers hurtle through the dark tunnel at an incredible speed and find themselves approaching a dazzling light, perhaps with a figure standing in it, welcoming them.

- They emerge into the light.

- A "being of light," known or unknown, may accompany the near-deathers on the rest of the journey. Sometimes the being appears to be a religious figure, such as Jesus, or it could be a deceased relative or friend. Small children describe meeting "a lady."

- Subjects enter a beautiful garden, where serene, soothing music plays. They often describe this as "heavenly" music.

- They may experience a panoramic life review (although this sometimes comes earlier), during which various scenes from their lives seem to pass before them, like sequences of a movie.

- Sometimes deceased friends and relatives visit them in a garden and give them information that later proves to be correct, including predictions regarding the future of the world.

- Subjects hear a voice telling them to return to life, or they are told to go back by one of the beings they have met. They often plead to be allowed to stay.

- The near-deather rapidly returns to his or her own apparently lifeless body, with all the attendant pain and discomfort of resuscitation.

- As a direct result of this experience, the near-deather's whole attitude to life changes. They become more interested in spiritual matters, although less dogmatically religious, and much less materialistic. They no longer have any fear of death.

Research shows that not all patients experience all the stages. In some 60 percent of the cases studied by Dr. Ring, the patients felt only the early stages of the "core experience," the blissful out-of-body sensations, before returning to normal consciousness.

Nevertheless, for most of them, even that was enough to transform them forever. []

A Conspiracy Theory
Paul McCartney Is Dead

Paul McCartney never wrote "Maybe I'm Amazed." He never formed the band Wings. He never clashed with Yoko, became a vegetarian, or fathered any of his children. When Queen Elizabeth knighted him in 1997, she was actually knighting someone else. This is because, conspiracy-minded Beatlemaniacs say, Paul McCartney secretly died in 1966. Theorists claim the other Beatles covered up his death — hiring someone who looked like him, sang like him, and had the same jovial personality. But the guilt eventually got to them and they began hiding clues in their music. In the song "Taxman," George Harrison gave his "advice for those who die," meaning Paul. The entire Sgt. Pepper's Lonely Hearts Club Band album was awash with Paul-is-dead clues: the Beatles had formed a "new" band featuring a fictional member named Billy Shears — supposedly the name of Paul's replacement. The album contained John Lennon's "A Day in the Life," which had the lyrics "He blew his mind out in a car" and the recorded phrase "Paul is dead, miss him, miss him," which becomes evident only when the song is played backward. Lennon also mumbled, "I buried Paul" at the end of "Strawberry Fields Forever" (in interviews, Lennon said the phrase was actually "cranberry sauce" and denied the existence of any backward messages).

Paul-is-dead believers think the Beatles accompanied these backward tape loops and veiled references to death with album covers that illustrated the loss of their friend. The original cover of 1966's Yesterday and Today album featured the Beatles posed amid raw meat and dismembered doll parts — symbolizing McCartney's gruesome accident. If fans placed a mirror in front of the Sgt. Pepper album cover, the words Lonely Hearts on the drum logo could be read as "1 ONE 1 X HE DIE 1 ONE 1." And of course, there's the Abbey Road cover, on which John, George and Ringo forwent all pretense and pretended to cross the street as a funeral procession. John wore all white, like a clergyman. Ringo, the mourner, dressed in black. George donned jeans, like a gravedigger. Paul wore no shoes (he didn't need them, because he was dead) and walked out of step with the others.

If Paul is dead, then his imposter is still at large. He met and married Linda Eastman, with whom he had four children before losing her to breast cancer in 1998. He released a live album in 1993 called Paul Is Live (likely story), and produced more than 20 solo albums — and that's not even counting the ones released by Wings. Then he endured a horrible divorce from Heather Mills, which may have made him wish he were dead — or, at least, were still Billy Shears. So who is the real McCartney? The world may never know.

The CIA and AIDS

Since the Centers for Disease Control and Prevention first reported the HIV/AIDS epidemic in 1981, rumors have persisted that the deadly virus was created by the CIA to wipe out homosexuals and African Americans. Even today, the conspiracy theory has a number of high-profile believers. South African President Thabo Mbeki once touted the theory, disputing scientific claims that the virus originated in Africa and accusing the U.S. government of manufacturing the disease in military labs. When she won the Nobel Peace Prize, Kenyan ecologist Wangari Maathai used the international spotlight to support that theory as well. Others insist that the government deliberately injected gay men with the virus during 1978 hepatitis-B experiments in New York, San Francisco and Los Angeles. Still others point to Richard Nixon, who combined the U.S. Army's biowarfare department with the National Cancer Institute in 1971. Though the co-discoverers of HIV — Dr. Robert Gallo of the National Cancer Institute and Dr. Luc Montagnier of the Pasteur Institute in Paris — don't agree on its origins, most members of the scientific community believe the virus jumped from monkeys to humans some time during the 1930s. []

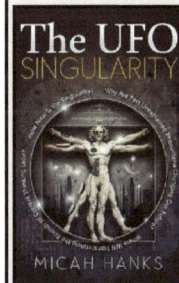

The Very First UFOs Were Terrestrial from Days of Old

In the 18th century inventors began to attach something heavy to a large amount of something lighter than air - hot air for example. Hot air balloons might have been invented as far back as 1709, by a Brazilian priest and inventor named Bartolomenu Lourenco de Gusmao. But it was closer to the end of that century before human beings began to fly, or at least to float through the air. In 1782, brothers Joseph and Etienne Montgolfier experimented with hot-air balloons in France. By 1783, they were ready to send up passengers - a rooster, a duck and a sheep! Everything went well, except for a minor injury to the rooster when the sheep kicked it. Next, the Montgolfier brothers sent up a man in a balloon that was tethered - attached to a line that remained firmly attached to the ground.

Then in November 1783, Jean Francois Piulatre de Rozier and the Marquis d'Arlandes wnet aloft, cut their balloon loose, and sailed over Paris at about 3,000 feet. Burning wool and straw to maintain a supply of hot air, they travelled for about 25 minutes and covered 5.5 miles. Delighted Parisians went into a frenzy over balloons. In fact balloon mania spread quickly and, all over Europe, people stitched up balloons and flew into the air.

In December 1783, inventor J.A.C. Charles flew a gas-filled balloon for two hours, covering 27 miles. The aging American philosopher-statesman (and inventor) Benjamin Franklin was in Paris at the time and called the flight "a most beautiful spectacle." Not everybody understood what all the fuss was about. Some asked Franklin what those floating things could possibly be used for. Franklin replied, "What use is a newborn baby?" But a use was soon found, in 1793 the first airmail letter was sent from London to Paris by balloon - the letter was addressed to B. Franklin.

Another American patriot, President Abraham Lincoln, got interested in balloons on June 17, 1861, when he received a telegraph message from high up in the air. A balloon enthusiast named Thaddeus Lowe had taken several representatives of the American Telegraph Company up over Washington, D.C., in a tethered balloon. They ran a wire down the tether and sent the first air-to-land telegram. It was forwarded to Lincoln.

That night Lowe's balloon was tethered on the White House lawn while Lincoln asked about military possibilities. During the war, Lowe gave valuable information to Union troops. Tethered balloons provided a high platform from which to spy on the enemy. As a psychological benefit, the balloons looked scary as they lurked above the battle zone. After trying unsuccessfully to shoot down Union balloons, the Confederacy decided they needed some of their own. They gave war that graceful Southern touch with silk balloon bags. This gave rise to the tale that Southern belles had dawned their best dresses to the air-war effort.

Inventors kept working on balloons. Heated air could get a balloon up, but the air cooled when the fuel ran out - and he balloon came down wherever it happened to be.

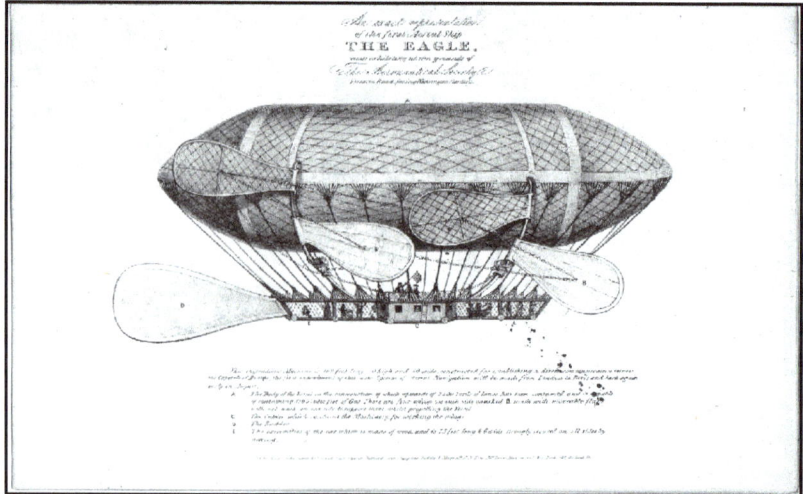

Keeping a fire going in the air was complicated and dangerous. Instead of warmed air, hydrogen gas - the lightest of the elements - worked well, though it was very flammable. Hydrogen was produced when a metal was dissolved in an acid. Sometimes other gases were used, such as coal gas used for lighting in some towns.

Unfortunately balloons still could not be steered. They could be made to go up by dropping ballast and down by letting out gas, but they had no controls for side-to-side motion or for speed. Off its tether, a balloon was at the mercy of the winds, and the "pilot" was just a passenger, which could quickly become an unhealthy situation. Inventors worked on devices to get the craft to go where the pilot wanted. They tried adding oars, sails, wings, parachutes, even propellers, but nothing worked. Someone suggested harnessing a team of vultures, but that didn't seem like a good idea. With limited success, the French tried a steam engine, human muscle power, and a small electric motor. In the late 1880s, Gottlieb Daimler's new lightweight gasoline engine changed everything. By the beginning of World War I, balloons were using motors, propellers and rudders, and venturing farther than ever before.

It is with the research above that I have been able to prove that the first sightings of UFOs in the United States were in fact "airships", piloted by human beings from planet Earth and not from the stars. []

Mr. President: If not America then who?
Continued From Page 32

I commend you for your action but I wonder how many thousands of people have been slaughtered by ISIS before this action and lay in trenches like the one shown in the photograph below all over western Iraq.

On June 14 almost a month a go this photograph was published on the web(http://rt.com/news/168916-isis-iraq-war-crimes/. This photo reminds me of the mass murder of the Jews by the Nazis in WW11. I believe that this was not an isolated incident but representative of what was and is taking place in those parts of Iraq attacked by ISIS.

I was just born at the end of WW11 so what I know about the Jewish holocaust is what I have seen in books, TV shows, and movies. As I watched the genocide in the security of my home I asked myself this question. Mr. President if not America than who? The world including America has watched for months the barbarian attacks by ISIS and yet no nation did anything. The only two nations that have some military resources that could have helped were France and England. One only has to look at the protests in the streets of London and Paris with the outbreak of hostilities between Israel and Hamas to see why neither nation wanted to get involved in Iraq. It seems the Muslims are powerful intimidators in those two countries and these nations could not come to the rescue.

I wonder how anybody regardless of religion or lack there of can look at this picture and not be shocked and outraged. Mr. President it appears that you have answered my question at least for now about providing for the people on the mountain food and water, but they can't live on top of the mountain forever. With in a few months the winter will come and it will be below freezing and a possible of snow. Will ISIS wait at the foot of the mountain for the people to come down looking for shelter from the cold with the trenches already dug like the one shown in the photo?

What is your long-term plan for the protection of the innocent or are you waiting for CNN to tell you Mr. President there is a problem.

Dan Perkins

Dan Perkins is a Registered Investment Advisor with over 40 years of money management experience and has written a trilogy on terrorism call the Brotherhood of the Red Nile. He can be contacted at his book web site www.danperkinsatsanibel.com.

Return Again

by
Georgina Cannon

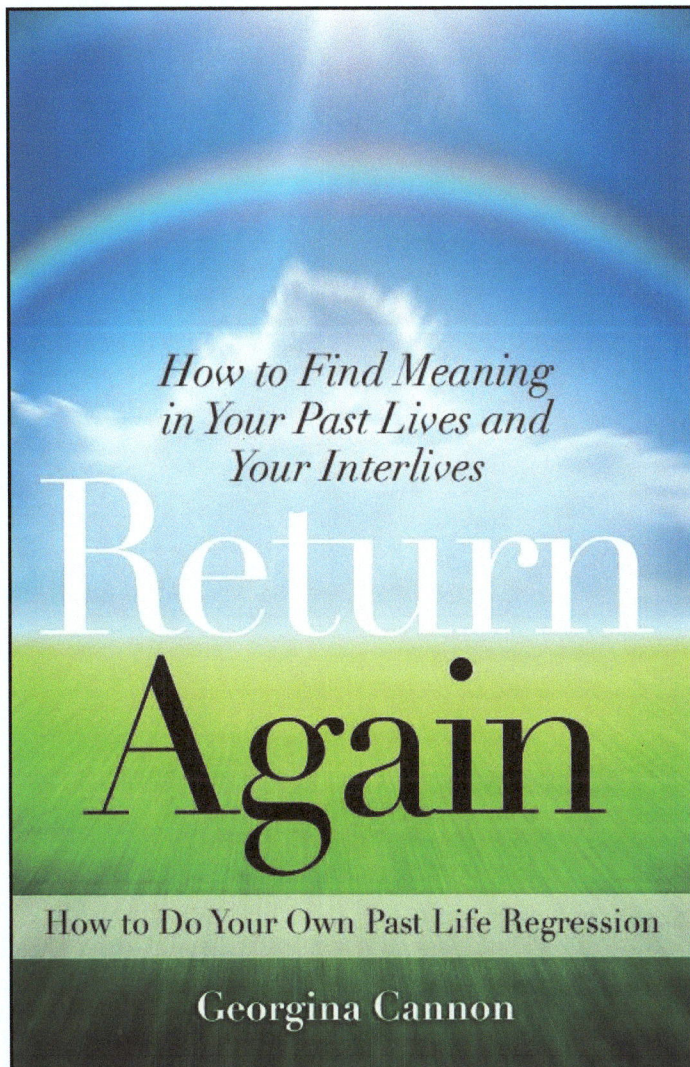

*How to Find Meaning
in Your Past Lives and
Your Interlives*

Return
Again

How to Do Your Own Past Life Regression

Georgina Cannon

Past Life and Interlife Regression Real or a Metaphor?

"With a journalism and corporate background, I'm not into the woo-woo of regression work" states Georgina Cannon, author, public speaker, clinician and hypnosis instructor.

"Return Again is my third book about the regression work – and believe me, I wouldn't be doing this if I didn't see the practical impact on the current life and research findings coming out of it"

For the past 17 years Cannon has been running Canada's largest hypnosis school and clinic, now focussing on her writing, she recalls the power of the work.

"In the Past Life Series I did for the CBC – PLI – Past Life Investigation, the researchers confirmed many of the lives of the 34 volunteers I worked with. And currently, my clients often verify the dates and events they experience in past lives. And even if they can't, or don't want to, the impact on their current life is profound and clarifying.

Whether you call the journey's Past Lives or a metaphor the mind makes up to give you the information – it really doesn't matter – I'm very pragmatic about this - what matters is that your current life is enriched from the knowledge and awareness of what is learned."

Dr Cannon's third book , RETURN AGAIN published by Red Wheel Weiser and is available at Amazon and local book stores.

ABOUT DR GEORGINA CANNON : Dr. Georgina Cannon is an award-winning board certified clinical hypnotist and was the founder of the Ontario Hypnosis Centre, She is recognized as the "public face" of hypnosis in Canada and a respected member of the mainstream health community. Dr. Cannon has been a frequent guest in the media, and her work and views have gained her prominence as a frequent source for news and feature articles on hypnosis and alternative therapies.

Before starting her hypnosis career in 1997, Georgina Cannon was the Managing Director, Senior Vice President of Burson-Marsteller Canada, responsible for the four offices in Canada and prior to that, the founder and General Manager of its spin-off, Cohn & Wolfe public relations. Georgina spent 23 years in corporate communications and journalism before making the decision to change careers.

Dr. Cannon is a regular public speaker and a featured lecturer at the University of Toronto's School of Social Work. Dr. Cannon has participated in Grand Rounds at Toronto hospitals, where she lectured to psychiatrists, physicians, nurses and social workers in the healing powers of hypnosis and regression work. Dr. Cannon has written and produced 25 self-hypnosis compact discs, 4 on line training DVD's.

www.georginacannon.com

INSTANT EVOLUTION
The Influence of the City on Human Genes
A Speculative Case

By
Howard Bloom

The dominant view in today's evolutionary psychology is that our instincts were stamped into our DNA during the infamous EEA, "The Environment of Evolutionary Adaptedness." This is generally reckoned as a roughly two and a half million-year hunter-gatherer phase that ended before the climax of the last Ice Age. Since then, our genetically preprogrammed heritage has supposedly been locked in stone (or better yet, in an amino acid code). We are, so says the current argument, tribal hunter-gatherers decked out in modern clothes.

However a strong case can be made for the possibility that human biology has continued to evolve during the ten thousand years since Jericho's builders erected the first city walls. Genes change far more speedily than most evolutionary psychologists realize. Natural selection has had 400 generations to rework our bodies and our brains since the days when Catal Huyuk, Suberde, and Tepe Yahya joined Jericho's mesh of intercity trade. Four thousand years before the rise of the Sumerian cities of Ur, Uruk, and Kish, Stone Age metropolises from Anatolia to the edges of India were already rich in challenges and opportunities. These urban traps and niches may well have been selectors forming much of what we are today. Homo urbanis has not only arrived, he has long since elbowed Homo tribalis far off to the side.

In 1979 University of Washington zoologist David Barash published a popular exposition of the then-new discipline of sociobiology called The Whisperings Within. [2] The book was rich in studies, theory, and in one of the most delicious forms of scientific sweets—illustrative anecdotes. As a companion piece to E.O. Wilson's original Sociobiology, [3] The Whisperings Within was a delight. [4] So when 1986 rolled around and Barash published yet another popular book, The Hare and the Tortoise: Culture, Biology, and Human Nature, [5] I dashed over to the Coliseum

bookshop in Manhattan and diligently hunted down a copy, then settled into a subway seat a few minutes later and prepared for a treat. What I got instead was a polemic, one in which references to research, to tales of animal behavior, and to a rich confection of anthropological surprises had ceased. Barash was now promoting a political agenda, one based on the notion that the evolution of human impulses had stopped long before the end of the last Ice Age. A living fossilization of the human brain, said Barash, was the source of many of our woes. We had the minds of cavemen but had fashioned ballistic-missile throwing stones complete with nuclear tips. Seized by caveman instincts, we were likely to bash each others' pates with our atomic clobberers, thus ending the brief existence of our oh-so-less-than-sapient human race.

The nuclear nightmare was very real when Barash penned this prose. Now that atomic weaponry has spread to countries like China, Pakistan, India, and such soon-to-be nuclear powers as Iran, Iraq, Libya, and North Korea, [6] the threat is even more real today. But the notion that our evolution came to a dead halt over ten thousand years ago seemed downright suspect. If moths in England could change the genes which color their wings in less than 50 years to blend in with the bark of pollution-blackened trees, · [7] why should we suppose that the inborn repertoire of feelings and behaviors on which human-ness is based was locked in Pleistocene chromosomes?

In the years since Barash issued his pronunciamento, the notion that we are hunter-gatherers in suits and ties has become common among evolutionary psychologists and numerous lay thinkers. In scholarly journals, popular magazines, and science specials on TV, it is popular to state that we are bearers of tribal instincts whose later immersion in agriculture, commerce, city living, and advanced technology hasn't done a bit to change our psychobiocircuitry. Jerome Barkow, Leda Cosmides, and John Tooby made this Pleistocene fixation campus dogma in their 1992 book The Adapted Mind. [8] Stephen Pinker, a scientist with smarts and current clout has said, " There's an endless [list] of things that we do that make no sense from a narrow

biological point of view. On the other hand, they do make sense when you recognize that every single one of them is a response to some recent bit of human technology that's been around for an eye blink in the human evolutionary scene, and that for the 99% of human existence in which we lived in nomadic hunter-gatherer bands, these temptations didn't exist. "And David Buss, another savvy thinker in the evolutionary explanation trade, has said point blank that we live "in the modern environment," but "we have a Stone Age brain. "

The real irony may be that David Barash proposed the notion of the Stone Age human psyche when he was moving from sociobiology into the field of peace studies. His formulation was designed to help us get a handle on our violent side. The gentling of humanity has not been the result. To the contrary. One of those who've echoed Barash's image of cavemen playing with plutonium was a truth-seeker holed up in a cabin near Lincoln, Montana, who wrote the following words: " I attribute the social and psychological problems of modern society to the fact that society requires people to live under conditions radically different from those under which the human race evolved. " The man who penned this statement and drew his inspiration from its point of view was Theodore Kaczynski, the Unabomber, who killed three people and injured 29 in the Ice-Age-and-savanna credo's name. [9]

What counts in science, however, is not a doctrine's political fruit, but the accuracy of its point of view. Do we really, as the title of one Australian Broadcasting Corporation special put it, have Stone Age Minds in Modern Skulls? [10] Are we tribal hunter-gatherers to the bone—or at least to the core of our neuronal wiring? I've been fortunate over the last four years to be allowed to review the record of human evolution from a heretic's perspective for a book John Wiley & Sons will publish this August—Global Brain: The Evolution of Mass Mind from the Big Bang to the 21st Century. uring the course of this reevaluation of evolutionary history I ran into a rather large surprise.

(Continued On Page 42)

Visit Howard Bloom Online
www.HowardBloom.net

Robert Lamar
Theatre of the Mind

Theatre of the MIND™ presents a tremendous collection of truly fascinating, yet totally unrehearsed, performances by volunteer audience members under the guidance of Robert LAMAR. These volunteers become the stars of this expertly produced presentation that should not be confused with what many would consider traditional hypnosis. Throughout Theatre of the MIND™, LAMAR invites his audience into a world where he encourages volunteers to enter a highly focused state of attention simply through applied suggestion. Perhaps, for the first time in their lives, participants let their hidden creative personalities leap to their full potential as LAMAR masterfully taps into their unexplored creativity. Volunteers may assume the persona of popular cultural icons like Elvis Presley, Michael Jackson, Madonna, Myley Cyrus or Justin Bieber. All of these pseudo stars may share the stage with another volunteer preoccupied with capturing a six foot grasshopper in one of many hilarious scenes.

The performances of the audience volunteers are completely unrehearsed. In fact, as Theatre of the MIND™ unfolds, it is very difficult to believe the participants are simply audience members. Because of this, each performance of Theatre of the MIND™ is totally unique. Every show is a one of a kind experience. In addition, a technically clever combination of music, lighting and special effects combine to create a modern show that appeals to today's audiences.

Theatre of the MIND™ is an original and a professional family show. Volunteers are not embarrassed or humiliated in any way, and all in attendance benefit from LAMAR's nearly three decades of study and experience in this specialized art. This is certainly one of Canada's most consistently acclaimed hypnotic attractions. Audiences are certain to be amazed whenever they enter Theatre of the MIND™.

ABOUT ROBERT LAMAR: Robert LAMAR has devoted much of his life to the study and understanding of magic, hypnosis, memory training and parapsychology. Born in the province of Ontario, Canada, he developed an interest in this specialized field at a very early age.

When he was just six he started learning the art of magic through trick packages he ordered from magic catalogues. When he was only twelve he saw one of the world's truly great entertainers, The Impossiblist, Peter Reveen. This event captivated the young Robert and he was further drawn by the power to perform and entertain. He eventually met Reveen and the friendship they established has endured for many years. He has also spent many years studying the allied arts, specifically mesmerism, hypnotism and magic as a performance art. His studies led him to the conclusion that the field he wished to enter was not one of formal hypnotism but that of a highly focused state of attention through which he could tap into a person's natural creativity. This was the formative basis for developing Theatre of the MIND™.

Robert LAMAR, in addition to more than thirty years devoted to the study of his craft, is a member of the International Brotherhood of Magicians (I.B.M.), a member of the Society of American Magicians and is also a member of the International Magic Society. The I.B.M. is the largest organization of its kind in the world. Membership is achieved only through sponsorship and Robert LAMAR's sponsor into the society was provided by his very good friend and mentor, Peter Reveen.

Tens of thousands of Canadians have been amazed and entertained by Theatre of the MIND™ through live shows and appearances on both CTV and CBC television. This is the signature of the most consistently praised hypnotic attraction.

www.RobertLamar.ca

INSTANT EVOLUTION
The Influence of the City on Human Genes
A Speculative Case
Continued From Page 40

The Stone Age was not entirely the property of nomadic hunting-gathering tribes. It also hosted the rise of the first cities. Much as I thought I'd been reasonably well educated in both biology and history, the notion that man had urbanized 5,000 years before the birth of Ur, Memphis, and Babylon came as rather a shock. Why had this not been taught in any of my courses in ancient history? What impact would an extra 100 generations of human life in the big burg and its countryside have on the evolutionary trajectory that has made us what we are today? Could it mean that we are not just men and women of the cave, the sabertooth, the mastodon, and the stone-flaked blade? Could it mean that some of us are something rather different—children of the alley, of the apartment, of the marketplace, and of the crowded downtown walkway?

The usual reason given for a no to questions of this sort is that, as John Tooby puts it : "Evolutionary change is very slow. " Altering the genome, we are told, takes hundreds of thousands or millions of years, not just decades or centuries. We could not possibly have undergone significant genetic reprogramming in the ten millennia since some of our ancestors left their tribal dwellings for the lure of the big city. So let's start by tackling the question of the speed limit on shape-shifting among genes. Indications are strong that human and non-human genes can alter in astonishingly short bursts of time. If this is true, and I hope to indicate it is, then many a human chromosome may have been recrafted by such forces of modernity as the city, long distance trade, and even the environments of nation states and of Imperial bureaucracies.

Geneticist Neil Howell, of the University of Texas' Galveston-based Medical Branch, contends that one form of human DNA—that contained in the mitochondria—sometimes makes adaptive shifts in a mere one or two generations. [11] The research with which he hopes to prove this is still in its infant stage. But Howell's suspicion that genes can be swift gains credibility from the rate of phenotypic change among insects and fish.

Here's an illustrative passage on the subject from my upcoming book, Global Brain: the Evolution of Mass Mind from the Big Bang to the 21st Century (John Wiley & Sons, August 2000):

If a passel of nearly identical animals is cooped up on a common turf, it frequently splinters into opposing groups which scramble determinedly down different evolutionary paths. E. O. Wilson, who brought attention to this phenomenon forty years ago, called it character displacement. [12] The battle over food and lebensraum compels each coterie to find a separate slot in the environment from which to chisel out its needs. [13] For example a small number of lookalike cichlid fish found their way to Lake Nyasa [14] in Eastern Africa roughly

12,400 years ago. It didn't take long for the finny explorers to overpopulate the place. As food became harder to find, squabbles and serious fights probably pushed the cichlids to square off in spatting cliques. The further the groups grew apart, the more different they became. [15] The details of this process are somewhat speculative, but the result is indisputable. The cichlids rapidly went from a single species of fish to hundreds, [16] each equipped with a crowbar to pry open opportunities others had missed. Some evolved mouths wide enough to swallow armored snails. Others generated thick lips to yank worms from rocks. One diabolical coven acquired teeth like spears, then skewered its rivals' eyeballs and swallowed them like cocktail onions. In the geologic blink of twelve thousand years, what had begun as a small group of carbon copies became 200 separate species–a carnival of diversity. [17]

Not only did twelve thousand years suffice to change the genes which gave these fish their body shape and bio-weaponry, that micro-sliver of an eon also provided ample time to rewrite the inborn script of fish psychology. Each new cichlid species was born chromosomally equipped with the hunting or scavenging instincts essential for its new specialty.

Then there's the swarm of bird-biting London mosquitoes which moved into the tunnels of the Underground in roughly 1900 when the city's half-built subway system was still occupied primarily by construction crews. Once below the sidewalk, the mosquitoes switched from feeding on feathered fliers to gorging on such delicacies as rats, straphangers, and maintenance workers. By the summer of 1998, the subterranean swarms had changed their genes so thoroughly that they could no longer mate with their distant relatives who lived above the pavement of the street. The pesky Tunnel bugs had taken their genome and gone off on their own, forming an entirely new species. [18] In reporting the story, Agence France Presse interviewed Roz Kidman Cox, the editor of BBC Wildlife Magazine, the publication responsible for initially breaking the news to a mass audience. Said Kidman Cox,

"The scientists we talked to say the differences between the above and below ground forms are as great as if the species had been separated for thousands of years, not just a century." [19] A mere one hundred years for a major shift in genes is not the painful crawl invoked by champions of Pleistocene fixation. Instead it is the quick-paced hop that Huxley called saltation. [20]

Yet another insect can change its genome twice that fast. It's the soapberry bug, which has renovated its chromosomes to fit new needs at a pace that's dizzying…taking not 100 years but a mere 50. From roughly 1900 to 1980 landscapers and city planners in Florida and in Louisiana produced a bonanza for any insect enterprising enough to go after it. The landscape designers imported new breeds of ornamental trees in an effort to help their clients outdo the neighbors or to spruce up a town's streets. Florida's sprucer-uppers chose the Golden Raintree (Koelreuteria elegans), which packaged its seeds in a slender pod whose walls were paper-thin. Louisiana's outdoor decorators went for Koelreuteria paniculata and Cardiospermum halicacabum, whose seeds were stashed in packets with far thicker casings. Soapberry bugs moved in to mine the new arboreal territories. Each developed genes for a proboscis appropriately sized to seize the opportunities. In Florida where the Raintree pods were easily pierced, the proboscises of soapberry bugs were short. This made for easy sipping, thus saving on resources and on energy. In Louisiana, where seeds of the new eye-pleasing trees were protected by thick rind, soapberry bugs developed a proboscis of a rather different kind—long, slender drilling cylinders which made the sipping rougher but could bore through sidewalls of a kind far tougher.

(Continued On Page 45)

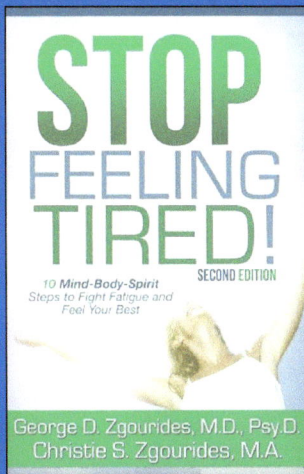

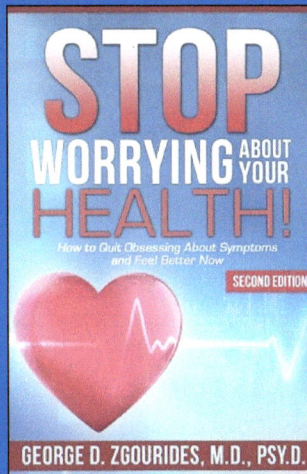

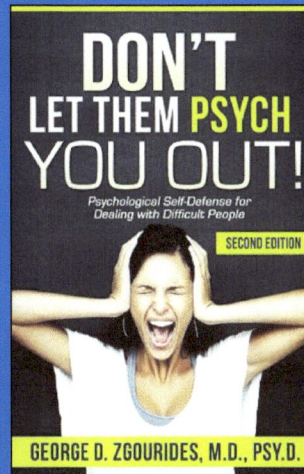

From Out of the Woodwork
A Tale of Ghostly Proportions
by
William S Peckham

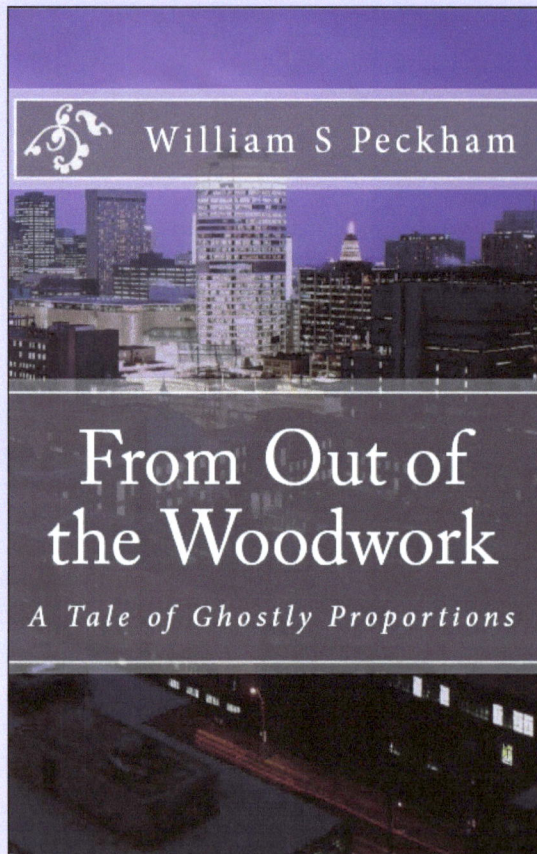

Some Of William's Many Reviews:

From Out of the Woodwork begins with a bang. The first line is an attention getter. The story is lively with action and colourful characters. One of the most tragic events of the 1900s is linked with one from the 2000s. It's a good read, with sprinkles of fun woven into some historic events that were not so fun.

- Dorothy Brotherton, Journalist, Kelowna BC.

I enjoyed the original way the author wove history into the story through the apparitions and his years in the home improvement field lends an air of authenticity to the story. It's for anyone who enjoyes a story with a touch of the paranormal and a mystery.

- Lisa Brandt, Broadcaster and Author of Venus Rising.

29 Livery Lane, a century house, once a house of some distinction and class now, fallen into disrepair, is purchased by Sean Kennedy. Sean, a contractor in Toronto, buys old houses, guts them and turns them into multi- family monstrosities... slums waiting to happen. When he starts work on his latest project, 29 Livery Lane, he encounters visions of former owners. At first, he is stunned by these apparitions, but as time moves on he welcomes them. Through these visions he learns about the house and some of the nine former owners. As a result of what he learns he decides to restore the old house not destroy it for profit.

The apparitions come to him when he touches books, reads letters, rummages through old boxes, finds a locket or reads a manuscript of a murder mystery. Through his many visions Sean gradually learns about the house, the way it looked in grander days and the fate of nine former owners, who left their indelible marks upon the house. The Phillips family, the original owners, left a story of love, closeness of family and a sea voyage, also the story of Stanley Renton, best-selling author, arrested for a murder which took place in the old house.

The story of the Kennedys, the present owners, is also one of love and family closeness and the deadly days of the terrorist's attacks on the Trade Centre Towers in New York, September 11, 2001.

Sean, through his research, meets Stanley Renton the only living, former owner. Sean and his family become very close friends with Stanley, during the restoration period.

When an apparition of a young mother and her daughter appears to Sean he figures that the daughter, Angelina Weston, could still be living and she might be able to shed some light upon the house and the way it looked. His meeting with Angelina turns into a warm friendship with this woman, now in her late eighties. The friendship blossoms and grows to include Stanley Renton as well.

The tales of the former owners lead Sean down many paths over a one-hundred-year period... from a trip on the St. Lawrence River in a small boat in the early 1900s to the recapture of a violent murderer in Niagara-on-the-Lake, in 2001.

The closing chapter of the book connects the Kennedys, the new owners, to the Phillips, the first owners. Stephen Phillips sends his wife and two children to Ireland to visit her mother and books their return on a cruise ship, April 10, 1912. Sean Kennedy also books a holiday for his wife and two children to visit her mother and father in England and then meet him in Boston, on September 10, 2001. Where they plan to continue on to Los Angeles and Disney Land the next day, September 11, 2001. Available on CreateSpace.com and Amazon.com.

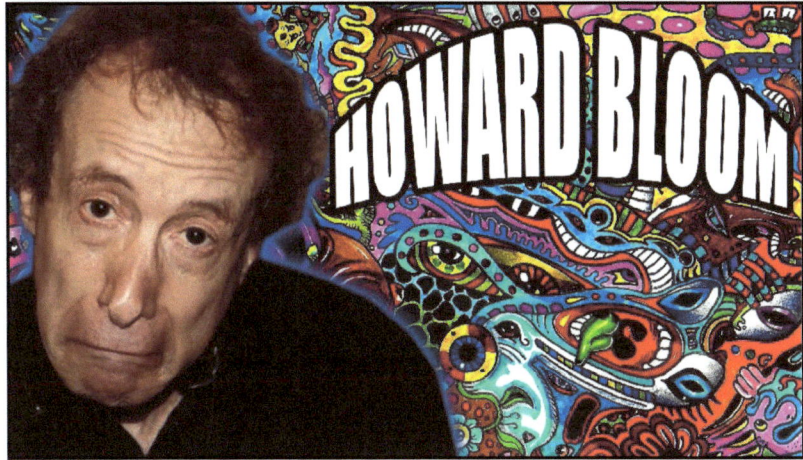

INSTANT EVOLUTION
The Influence of the City on Human Genes
A Speculative Case
Continued From Page 42

Was this really a genetic alteration, or had soapberry bugs whose proboscises were already short or long simply moved long distances, each to the appropriate destination. Genetic testing showed that the specialized bugs had not come from far away, but had evolved from local insects whose proboscises had previously been adapted to harvest the bounty only of the local trees. By checking the dates at which the new greenery had ben brought in, researchers could pinpoint the time it had taken to tweak genes for proboscis length. That span turned out to be a breathlessly brief half a century. [21] So a flick of reproductive time can remake genomes in fast-breeding bugs, but what about in larger beings?

In the 1970s, Thomas and Amy Schoener [22] deliberately stranded Anolis sagrei lizards from Staniel Cay on numerous smaller islands in the Bahamas, each with a different sort of foliage. Lizards on islands with stumpy plants adorned with small leaves can operate more efficiently with short hind legs. Lizards on islands whose plants are larger and more luxuriant do better if they have the long legs perches on large leaves and large plant trunks allow, since long legs also increase escape speed when running from the local lizard eaters. Washington University biologist Jonathan B. Losos predicted that over time natural selection would prune the lizards' genes to equip the scattered creatures with the limbs which best fit their needs. But how much time would genetic pruning take? Return trips to the islands revealed it hadn't taken much time at all. The lizards on each island were soon measurably different. Some managed to diverge genetically from their parent strain in the twitch of a single decade. That's the equivalent of ten generations—200 years—in human time.

Yet according to University of Washington evolutionary ecologist John N. Thompson, even this genetic sprint is painfully slow. Says Thompson, "dozens" of genetic transmutations have been known to take place in a matter of mere decades. [23] Thompson backs up his claims with rather startling facts:

· *"Gene-for-gene coevolution in wild flax and flax rust in Australia has produced large changes in allele frequencies within and among populations over just the past decade alone*

· *"The frequency of clones in Potamopyrgus antipodarum snails within a single lake in New Zealand has changed within the past decade through time-lagged selection imposed by a major trematode parasite.*

· *"The introduction of myxoma virus into Australia as a biological control agent against rabbits resulted in rapid evolution toward decreased virulence within only a few years."* [24]

Thompson explains that one cause of swift genetic change is the sort of race in which one species has to keep pace with its enemies and ecological partners. And lizard expert

Jonathan Losos adds that, " If colonizing populations are displaced into an environment that is often very different from that of their source, they are particularly likely to diverge evolutionarily. " What's more, writes Losos, the greater the difference in habitat, "the greater the magnitude of differentiation."

Both these spurs to genetic speed were at work in the post-glacial paradise of the Near East. It is difficult to find a human habitat more strikingly different from those which came before than that created by the city. It is also hard to find an environment in which the race against the neighbors could have been quicker. Times were turbulent during the Pleistocene, and there is evidence that neolithic tribes were subject to attack by murderous rivals. [25] A bewildering variety of proto-hominids lived, for example, in Northern Spain's Atapuerca 800,000 years ago. We know little about their way of life, but the clues to their way of death indicate that they may have been carved and eaten by whatever fellow humans did them in. [26]

Neanderthals were not the gentle hominids pictured in the novels of Jean Auel. One hundred twenty to eighty thousand years ago, some apparently lived on a diet of red deer...and of other Neanderthals. [27] That was a long time ago. But 100,000 years later the Neolithic Anasazi, the Aztecs, and the late Stone Age occupants of Fiji were still munching on the members of enemy tribes. (This gives the old song "Love Me Tender" an entirely new meaning.)

There's no sign of this cannibalism in the Near East—but its mere existence is testament to the lack of interhominid peace. During the late Pleistocene, men attained the ability to attack each other with much more than just the stone axe, the spear, [28] and ravenous teeth. [29] Reports military historian Arther Ferrill, the bow may have been invented as long as 50,000 years ago, as was an even more formidable weapon, the sling. Bows "more than doubled the range of a spear," and arrows were far more portable than the spear had been. But slings such as those we see in nightly news reports of Palestinian street demonstrations trumped the bow's advantages handily. They had greater range and accuracy than arrows, and could be more deadly, even smashing through armor. Ferrill has no doubt that these weapons, along with the dagger and the mace, were used by groups of late Stone Age humans to assault

the neighbors, and to do so with grim regularity. He says:

In prehistoric times man was a hunter and a killer of other men. The killer instinct in the prehistoric male is clearly attested by archaeology in fortifications, weapons, cave paintings, and skeletal remains. ... Neolithic cave paintings show warriors forming a line, firing on command, and marching in column behind a leader who was wearing a distinctive uniform that distinguished him from the rest of his troops. ... [In the Egyptian site known as 'cemetery 117,' which was actively used from 12,000 to 4,500 BC] nearly half of the fifty-nine skeletons show signs of violent deaths inflicted by small flake points (microliths), probably arrowheads. Some of the dead suffered from multiple wounds, and points were discovered in the sphenoid bones in two skulls, suggesting that the victims were shot under the lower jaw, probably as they writhed in pain on their backs. A young adult female had twenty-one stone artifacts in her body. [30]

Late Ice Age tribes had depended on state-of-the-art wooden ramparts to ward off murderous attacks. [31] But once the glaciers had peeled back and left an unbelievable garden of edible plants and equally delectable animals on the Eden-like plains East of the Mediterranean and the Aegean Sea, men and women presumably had the spare time to think up a more ingenious form of defense. The first great leap forward appeared in the form of Jericho, a city conceived and built a full 10,000 years ago when most humans were still living in huts and caves. Jericho's advances in military technology were light years ahead of anything which had come before. The city's mortarless boulder bastions, were 6.5 feet thick and four times the height of a Neolithic man.

(Continued On Page 48)

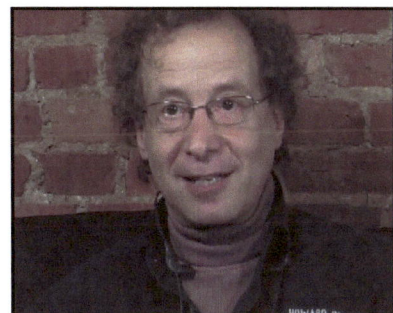

You Can Make A Real Change in 2014!

You can change non-productive patterns of behavior!
You can change negative thinking and the related stress it brings!

STOP STRUGGLING !

FIND AND CHANGE WHAT IS HOLDING YOU BACK...

If you are ready for changes in your life then Me Sah, Spiritual Medium, Clairvoyant, Inner Energy Coach and Healer can help you to:

- Discover how to heal, grow, and expand your awareness.
- Create positive emotional, mental and physical energy patterns.
- Improve performance and confidence in all endeavors...sports, school, relationships, work and more.
- Advance your Spiritual development.
- Improve relationships.
- Make connections with loved ones who have passed.
- Find your life's purpose and direction.
- Understand the close relationships with your pets.

An Authentic Experience: Me Sah, a Spiritual Medium/Clairvoyant, Counselor and Energy Coach from Santa Fe, New Mexico, has attained a highly attuned level of connection to Spirit and the Angelic Realms. With her help you can experience enlightenment and expand your level of awareness.

For over 40 years Me Sah has been not only a spiritual teacher and consultant but a student of Spirit, metaphysics, spirituality, meditation, phenomenon, and the esoteric. As a medium, spiritual reader and guide, animal communicator, healer, and a metaphysical Priest she helps others make a connection to the greater consciousness of their being.

Me Sah has a Masters of Social Work degree and has worked as a psychotherapist. She has been trained in crisis intervention, drug abuse, and family therapy. She is a Certified Matrix Energetics Practitioner and is also certified in the Whitehawk Process. In addition, she has been certified in Educational Kinesiology (Whole Brain Integration and Learning) and functioned as a practitioner, teacher and consultant. Mesah utilizes various other alternative processes. New techniques and understandings are continually being transmitted directly through Spirit. She was ordained as a metaphysical Priest in 1976 and as a non-denominational minister in 2000.

Daily she deals with situations concerning dysfunctional energy patterns, non-physical beings, animal companions, entities and more. With a direct link to Spirit, one of the most important aspects of her work is to help people cross over and to help those who have left their physical bodies but are stuck between realms. Helping guide them to the Light gives them peace as well as to those left behind in the physical dimension.

www.mesah.weebly.com

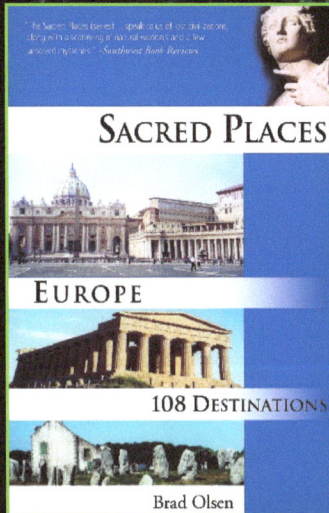

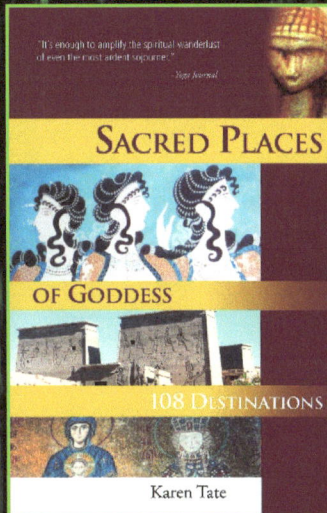

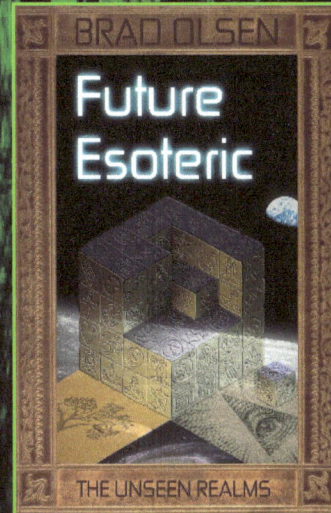

INSTANT EVOLUTION
The Influence of the City
on Human Genes
A Speculative Case
Continued From Page 45

They were surrounded by a trench nine feet deep and 27 feet wide guarded by watchtowers an unbelievable three stories high. Evolution works by weeding out weakness and favoring strength. A city with a wall like this gained a titanic edge in the times' arms race.

Which brings us back to the words of biologist Jonathan Losos " If colonizing populations are displaced into an environment that is often very different from that of their source, they are particularly likely to diverge evolutionarily. " The environment of Jericho was very different indeed. [32] Unlike previous fortifications, the city's walls were apparently not built to cut off and protect the members of one tribe. On the contrary, scholars who have studied the place claim that Jericho was constructed to attract strange foreigners and other passersby. The city was an oasis designed to provide water and shelter to a steady flow of traders.

Trade was also a major raison d'être for another city hundreds of miles north on the Anatolian plains, a town of roughly 60,000 inhabitants which has left highly instructive remains. This was Catal Huyuk, [33] a mass of low slung apartment buildings which came to life roughly 8,000 years ago. Which brings us to another evolutionary argument. Those who regard agriculture and modernity as the source of all human woes have frequently contended that cities did not confer selective advantages, instead they were selective liabilities. Say the naysayers of the polis, dependence on single-crop diets and the crowding of urban life produced everything from plague and dental cavities to a dramatically shortened life. [34] Cities, they say did not breed a new kind of human being, instead it bred its citizens out. Towns lost inhabitant so quickly to disease that they constantly needed to replenish their population with newcomers from the countryside. [35] Hence natural selection favored rural types reproductively but turned thumbs down on those lured by the high jinks of the city. [36]

But late Stone Age city dwellers were not limited to murderous diets of carbohydrates. Early cities like Jericho and Catal Huyuk were apparently not based on the new trick of planting yourself in one spot and poking seeds into the ground, then waiting until they sprouted and digging up the edible bulbs or lopping off the starchy tops. Nor were the first towns based on domesticating the wild game that wandered on the grasslands close at hand. Evidence suggests that the new cities were founded on hunting and gathering, but without the old-fashioned wandering. Urban centers like Catal Huyuk and Jericho initially took their nourishment from a surrounding overflow of wild grain and game spiced with the gastronomic joys provided by the era's booming trade.

Dining in these Stone Age cities was

very rich indeed. Fourteen different kinds of food nourished the residents of Catal Huyuk 8,500 years ago. The standard groceries ranged from meat and cereals to berries and nuts. This means the citizens were better nourished than tribal hunter gatherers. One of the main urban staples was red deer, whose herds were so abundant that the reliability of their presence is strongly indicated by both the kitchen middens and the elaborate murals daubed on the walls of Catal Huyuk's standardized, one-plan-fits-all, three-room flats. A huge percentage of those paintings celebrate the joys hunting parties of men took in bringing down does, fawns, and bucks with arrow and bow. Archaeological remains also indicate the many non-culinary ways in which trade boosted the quality of life in Catal Huyuk dramatically. To quote from an early draft of Global Brain:

The fir from which were carved the elegant adornments gracing sacred alters and the best homes came from the Taurus mountains, as did epicurean delicacies like almonds, pistachio, apples, acorns (good not only for feed but as raw material for leather tanning chemicals and for yogurt making), and berries like juniper and the wine makers' favorite, hackberry. Other mountains closer by provided greenstone, limestone and volcanic rock. Catal Huyuk's alabaster and calcite came from Kayseri, and its creamy white marble from lands far to the west. Its cinnabar was imported from Sizma, and its shells from Mediterranean beaches many miles and mountain ranges to the south. Salt, one of the greatest lacers of distant cultures into nets of trade, came from Ihcapmar, whose industry was based on the mineral gifts of a nearby brackish lake.

The numerous sources from which the citizens of Catal Huyuk purchased their delicacies and building materials gives a rough idea of the number of other towns built around trade. More important, it indicates how much better housed were the members of Catal Huyuk than those who still lived in the old tribal ways. Cities provided protection from cold, rain, and, according to the anthropologists studying the sites, even from natural disaster. Archaeological reasoning says that because of the variety of their resources and of their specialist's abilities,

towns could recover from flood or earthquake far more rapidly than tribes still following herds of reindeer or guarding a pass through which other migratory animals flowed.

Urban advantages were so numerous that archaeological remains demonstrate the following fact with overwhelming clarity: tribe after tribe deserted its previous home to migrate en masse into the cities, [37] swelling their population and adding to their diversity.

My admittedly group-oriented theory of evolution--whose model was introduced in my previous book, The Lucifer Principle: a scientific expedition into the forces of history, [38] and is amplified significantly in my new volume, Global Brain--places a premium on the potential phylogenetic effects of inter-group tournaments—battles between tribes, city states, nations, and nearly every other form of social gang. Urban populations have been winning battles, establishing empires, and subjugating country folk for ten thousand years now. The natural selection which winnows social entities has favored city dwellers so powerfully that "indigenous" tribal folk are now on the endangered cultures list. Their hunter-gatherer mode of organization has been tested and has proven wanting. The real irony is that today hunter-gatherers are being "saved" by the surplus time and energy city life grants to its intellectual elites. Only these highly-educated beneficiaries of the interurban weave have sufficient resources to mount the crusades which currently are attempting to keep societies that failed alive.

(Continued On Page 51)

RAZOR OF MADNESS

Wayne Morin, Jr and Thomas Lee Howell

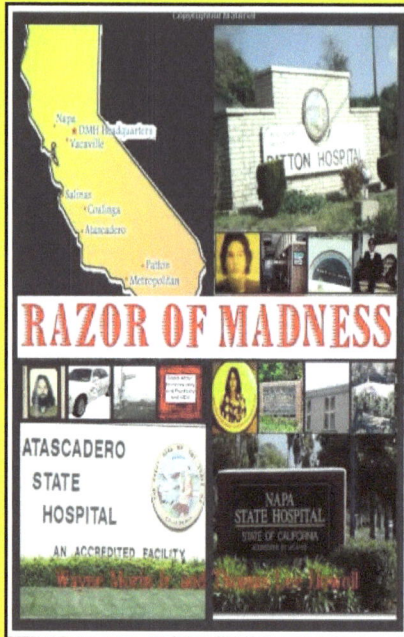

ABOUT THE AUTHOR - WAYNE MORIN, JR.

Wayne Morin Jr. is a real life Crusader and Guardian Angel for those clients and patients who are behind the walls of Napa State Hospital still suffering at the hands of those who are supposed to protect and care for them.

The State of California held him incarcerated in jails and mental institutions since he was a homeless teenager at 14 until his release as a mature adult in 2003. Abuse, drug addiction, rape, and murder are all a part of Wayne's story and observations of his time spent in mental hospitals. While he was at Napa State Hospital Wayne was encouraged by his doctor, psychologist and ConRep to stop exposing atrocities at Napa State Hospital for one year which Wayne had been doing by sending letters to news media. He was told to concentrate on his S.A.F.E Program. His ConRep told Wayne he would allow him to expose the information he was already doing at Napa State once he was back in the community. He said that while President Clinton was in office that he made it impossible for clients to pursue criminal actions while at state mental hospitals.

Once the client had been released, he would be able to have their complaints heard by proper authorities. They spoke in detail until the ConRep understood his reasons for exposing the hospital.

Once Wayne knew that the ConRep had his best interests at heart and was not lying about his criminal background, Wayne was able to trust him.

That ConRep worker is a big part of what he is today, and is a role model for all mental health workers. His honesty and understanding of Wayne's abandonment from childhood made their connection real.

Once Wayne left Napa State he started producing TV programs and radio talk shows about the criminal activity at Napa State Hospital. Wayne found out how to become a law abiding citizen. His ConRep helped him find living arrangements making sure that Wayne was in some sort of recovery program for either drugs or alcohol. He helped him find work and they became best friends. A few years ago Wayne went in front of the Napa County Courts to ask for his release from ConRep. Wayne's ConRep and doctors were all onboard with this decision. Wayne feels that by state standards was restored to sanity. He now lives right on Napa State Hospital grounds - not on the property but can look out his back window and see the units he was on at the age of 13 years old.

Wayne Morin Jr. is a success story. He has been in recovery from 7-15-03 in a 12 step program. Wayne loves being free and the beautiful Napa Valley California. He has many people who care about him today and truly feels the same for them. Wayne will continue to bring light to the crimes that to this very day go unpunished at Napa State Hospital.

To purchase your copy of RAZOR OF MADNESS, visit Wayne's website at www.waynemorinjr.com.

RAZOR OF MADNESS is also available at CreateSpace.com and Amazo.com in Print & Kindle versions.

www.WayneMorinJr.com

INSTANT EVOLUTION
The Influence of the City on Human Genes
A Speculative Case
Continued From Page 48

Meanwhile 27 million people, many of whom have chosen to escape one of their country's 48 surviving tribes, [39] are gathered in one town alone—Mexico City. These have managed to outbreed and far outlive their very distant hunting/gathering relatives still barely clinging to the ancient ways of life along the banks of the Amazon River and the Orinoco. True, many live in shanties and send their children out to gather food and other necessities from garbage piles we see as a living hell. But in hunter-gatherer terms, these trash heaps are a treasure trove. Yes, I am saying that even a city's scraps can provide a more nourishing and reliable source of food than natural, organic fare tracked down in the wilderness. Primatologist Shirley Strum's baboons managed to demonstrate this fact. The Pumphouse Gang of baboons Strum studied in Kenya eventually broke up into several factions. One stuck to the good old hunter-gatherer ways—digging in almost-impossibly hard soil to pull wild bulbs from the ground and occasionally eating meat when they could bring a young gazelle or other animal down. Others moseyed over to a nearby army barracks and rummaged for food in the place's large trash pile. Those which stuck to grubbing for all-natural groceries were only able to produce new infants every eighteen months and showed the scruffy signs of marginal health. But the breakaway young Turks who learned to find their sustenance in the military garbage dump grew large and muscular. They were well nourished and well rested when it came time for the troops to fight. When battle came it was usually they who attacked. Meanwhile their females could birth new babies at mere twelve-month intervals, a remarkable reproductive luxury. When Strum's vets subjected the garbage pickers and the ground-scrabbling traditionalists to medical tests, the health of the rubbish-relishers was so robust it made the physical fitness of those who'd stuck to a natural diet seem pathetic at the very best. [40]

Historical surveys of health among Native Americans··· in the days before Columbus arrived indicate that the hunter-gatherer life hasn't been any kinder to humans than it has been to baboons. Biological historian Suzanne Austin Alchon reports that among New World hunter-gatherers:

Life expectancies at birth were short... from 16 to 22 years for males and 14 to 18 years for females.... This meant that few lived long enough to develop chronic, degenerative diseases associated with aging.... At least 40 percent of all children died by age 5. Complications due to childbirth were a leading cause of death among women. Males, on the other hand, were more likely to sustain traumatic injuries either as a result of violence or accident.... 'Cannibalism, infanticide, sacrifice, geronticide, head-hunting, and other forms of warfare,' was common in many hunter-gatherer societies. ... Among the diseases common to hunter-gatherer populations... [were] bacterial and parasitic infections such as shigellosis, salmonellosis, tapeworms, hookworms, whipworms, and pin worms,... helminthic infections such as tapeworms,... bacterial diseases, staphylococcal and streptococcal... amebiasis, giardiasis, and toxoplasmosis, all protozoan infections... New World leishmaniasis and American trypanosomiasis, or Chagas' disease... New World spotted fever... bartonellosis, or Carrion's disease, transmitted by sandflies, ... other spirochetal diseases, leptospirosis and two types of relapsing fever... anemia, meningitis, or hemorrhaging ... [and] endemic relapsing fever [whose] louse-borne epidemic variety... could produce mortality rates of up to 50 percent.

One result: among "small, mobile populations ...most individuals were under the age of 20." Another: "In spite of poor nutrition and rising rates of infection, sedentary populations throughout the Americas expanded over time... the availability of corn pap allowed mothers to wean their children at an earlier age, thus decreasing the time between birth intervals. This allowed women to bear more children over the course of their reproductive lives." [41] In other words, the sedentary New World farmers and the city dwellers whom they fed passed the ultimate evolutionary test. They outbred their wandering tribal neighbors and subjugated them militarily.

As the history of the Olmec, Toltec, Maya, Inca, and Aztec attest, in the post-Jericho world even tillers of the soil would be drawn into the city's sway, altering their crops and ways of life to fit a sprawling metro-based economy. Or, to put it differently, the rise of the city radically changed the playing field even for those who resolutely planted themselves in the distant countryside. And Darwin tells us it's this sort of social makeover whose pressures do the most to pick and choose new crops of genes. [42]

Human genetic updates snap into place far more rapidly than we think. Here's another tidbit from the pages of Global Brain:

Behold the refinement of the LA gene which confers the ability to digest milk on adults. Some people, notably those of Northern Europe, ·· [43] have it. Others–like East Asians and Polynesians–don't. It's particularly handy in wintry climes, where the sun frequently refuses to reveal enough of its radiance to generate Vitamin D in human skin. This is a deficiency which cow's milk neatly cancels out. [44] However humans... probably didn't domesticate animals from which they could derive dairy drinks until after the first cities were founded. Which means the gene for adult milkshake tolerance did not appear until well after the walls of Jericho were erected and Bos taurus [the nine-foot-tall wild bull from which most domesticated cattle descend] was taught to toe the line. Other genes have arisen during this geological wink of time. [45] One is the sickle cell anemia gene which a mere 2,000 years ago [46] began protecting black Africans against malaria. [47] Still more are found in the immune shields which defended the European conquerors of the Americas from scourges like measles and smallpox. This heritage of disease resistance seems to have begun in the last five thousand years or less and developed to its fullest just within the last millennium. One clue to the immunological recency: measles is thought to have jumped to humans from the rinderpest of domesticated cattle. [48] It was the dense-packed urban environment which turned it to a killer. [49] In the grisly manner evolution favors, the measles virus massacred those in European cities who had no genetic resistance and left only the fortunates whose genes were able to adjust the immune system to mount an appropriate defense. These protective genes then grew robust within the following generations, making a profound mark on the face of history. The genetic acquisition of immunity was the greatest weapon of the Conquistadors and colonialists, who wiped out an estimated seventy million Native Americans * with the unseen weapons of their germs. [50]

(Continued On Page 52)

INSTANT EVOLUTION
The Influence of the City on Human Genes
A Speculative Case
Continued From Page 51

Other selective pressures for biological change have run rampant since the days when men first invented the temptation of the city. Most of these pressures are of the sort most likely to shape brain physiology and lead to the creation of "mental modules" oriented toward large-scale social integration. The slice of mankind which pioneered the use of cities in the late Stone Age steeped itself in an urban environment for a good 5,000 years before the more famous cities like Ur, Babylon, and Thebes kicked off the later phases of the metropolitan experience. During that pre-Ur stage, the remains of Catal Huyuk make it clear that social differentiation was strong. It appears that wealth was shuttled massively toward those who specialized in the perpetuation and regeneration of large-scale social dynamics. Priests, for example, are specialists in social cohesion. The work of anthropologist Mary Douglas hints that religious rituals may be practice for the routines which pin together a society. [51] Rituals inculcate obedience to authority, and act as calisthenics for the sort of simultaneous, coordinated activities—complete with selfless sacrifice–which make massive social structures tick. Confucius would have agreed. To him, the constant exercise of ritual was an indispensable social need. Try thinking of it this way: civility is a set of habits, habits of cooperation and habits of self-restraint. To attain these civilized disciplines, one needs a strong prefrontal cortex—home of the executive functions that rein our more chaotic impulses in. One also needs practice—practice repeated nearly every day. Regular rehearsal keeps the habits of self-control vigorously alive. Religious rituals are calisthenics for the habits indispensable to large-scale social enterprise.

Religion also keeps our ancestors chorusing inside of us, inculcating wisdom garnered long before we were born. It links us to the data base of generations which have come before. Supercomputers of the late '90s pulled off superhuman feats with a mere dozen processing units hooked up as a team. If a group of 50 humans makes up its mind by parallel processing, that's 50 processors in the neural net at any given time. But add the memory stores of 50 generations, and you've plugged vestiges of output from 24,950 modules more into your processing line.

Ancestor worship and respect for ancient authority are among the few things which separate man from beasts. They link us in a chain of wisdom which transcends the centuries. In Catal Huyuk, those who ran the rituals and vivified the myths behind them were the city's priests. So heavily did Catal Huyuk rely on the social glue of priestly ritual that one room in every three was a holy sanctuary. For their services priests were given larger living spaces, more generous allotments of food, and numerous other luxuries. If disaster struck, priests were among the best placed to survive.

So were other experts in social connectivity—political leaders like kings, judges, and military chiefs able to settle disagreements with a minimum of friction, to boost consensus, to give men confidence in times which made them tremble, to advance a city's interests, and to help it dodge catastrophe. Merchants tied a city's market to the sources of the goods which satisfied the populace's hungers for basics and for luxuries. These wheeler-dealers pulled together webs of commerce whose furthest ends were hundreds, and later thousands, of miles away. (Catal Huyuk's lapis lazuli came 1,500 miles from southern Russia.)

The rich of neolithic cities were the masters of human synapsing. When times turned mean and the deprived were faced with death, the rich were those most likely to survive. Their progeny were blessed with the ability to win the finest mates and to make sure that, in their turn, their children thrived. A city favored those who mastered it. It gave a reproductive edge to those whose genes had helped them plait the social weave. And it favored good followers as well, those able to tame their "primitive" instincts and to demonstrate civility. In times of famine or of drought when the poor curled up in the streets and died, those who led or who obeyed were those most likely to remain alive.

The form of disaster which winnows phenotypes struck cities over and over again. It struck in the form of war—a variety of misfortune which would inspire human ingenuity to create offensive weapons and clever stratagems able to undo the invincibility of a rival city's bastions. Jericho would tumble (literally—the city's walls collapsed a total of seven times) and the first metropolis of all would become a wasteland for thousands of years while rival cities thrived. The same fate would befall the early cities of the Indus Valley's Harappan civilization. To the best and most cleverly organized went the spoils--one of which included the continued power to be fruitful and multiply. Thus obedience, cleverness, and organizational creativity thrived. It was literally bred in to the post-Neolithic form of Homo sapiens.

Then there were the post-agricultural plagues, which continued to decimate populations from Biblical times through Athens' glory days, the height of the Renaissance and the Age of Reason, on up to the influenza pandemic of 1919. In these, the rich outlasted the poor. As Boccaccio demonstrated in The Decameron, when others were falling in the streets, the wealthy escaped the cities' ills by high-tailing it to their fancy country retreats. In some cases the rich even benefitted from a scourge, as did the founder of the Krupp fortune, a wealthy burgher during the Black Death who bought up scads of homes and farms left vacant by plague-eradicated families. In normal time these buildings and their fields would have cost a fortune. But in the wake of the bubonic curse they were literally available for pennies. Krupp's legacy (and progeny) prosper off his callous canniness to this very day. But above all, it was, as I said, those who had mastered the art of social integration who were privileged to protect themselves through superior nourishment, housing, and other services from the probability of death. These included statesmen (masters of such cohesive skills as horse-trading, persuasion, and coalition building), warrior-heroes-turned leaders (masters of survival in intergroup tournaments), and wealthy merchants (knitters of intergroup links).

Plagues came over and over again. So did war. Each ran humanity through a selective sieve, culling out the socially unskilled from those who had mastered the large scale urban environment. There have been enormous disputes over the reasons for genetic change in Europe during the post-Neolithic age. Between them, investigators like Ammerman, Cavalli-Sforza, Renfrew, Barbujani, Jacquez, Ligi, Calafell, Bertranpetit, Derish, Sokal, Moral, Marogna, Salis, Succa, Vona, Piazza, Cappello, Olivetti, and Rendine have subjected nearly a thousand different European alleles to scrutiny . But one thing all the disputants agree on is that change has occurred genetically, and that it's happened massively. [52] Would some mental modules be favored and others suppressed by 500 generations of this post-urban process? I suspect the answer would be yes. The mental twists most likely to have been blessed were those for living in the city.

(Continued On Page 53)

INSTANT EVOLUTION
The Influence of the City on Human Genes
A Speculative Case
Continued From Page 52

About Howard Bloom

"I know a lot of people. A lot. And I ask a lot of prying questions. But I've never run into a more intriguing biography than Howard Bloom's in all my born days." Paul Solman, Business and Economics Correspondent, PBS NewsHour

Howard Bloom has been called "next in a lineage of seminal thinkers that includes Newton, Darwin, Einstein,[and] Freud," by Britain's Channel4 TV , "the next Stephen Hawking" by Gear Magazine, and "The Buckminster Fuller and Arthur C. Clarke of the new millennium" by Buckminster Fuller's archivist. Bloom is the author of The Lucifer Principle: A Scientific Expedition Into the Forces of History ("mesmerizing"—The Washington Post), Global Brain: The Evolution of Mass Mind from the Big Bang to the 21st Century ("reassuring and sobering"—The New Yorker), The Genius of the Beast: A Radical Re-Vision of Capitalism ("Impressive, stimulating, and tremendously enjoyable." James Fallows, National Correspondent, The Atlantic), and The God Problem: How A Godless Cosmos Creates ("Bloom's argument will rock your world." Barbara Ehrenreich).

Bloom has been published in arxiv.org, the leading pre-print site in advanced theoretical physics and math. He was invited to tell an international conference of quantum physicists in Moscow in 2005 why everything they know about quantum physics is wrong. And his book Global Brain was the subject of an Office of the Secretary of Defense symposium in 2010, with participants from the State Department, the Energy Department, DARPA, IBM, and MIT.

Bloom has founded three international scientific groups: the Group Selection Squad (1995), which fought to gain acceptance for the concept of group selection in evolutionary biology; The International Paleopsychology Project (1997), which worked to create a new multi-disciplinary synthesis between cosmology, paleontology, evolutionary biology, and history; and The Space Development Steering Committee (2007), an organization that includes astronauts Buzz Aldrin, Edgar Mitchell and members from NASA, the National Science Foundation, and the Department of Defense.

Bloom explains that his focus is "mass behavior, from the mass behavior of quarks to the mass behavior of human beings." In 1968 Bloom turned down four fellowships in psychology and neurobiology and set off on a science project in a field he knew nothing about: popular culture. He was determined to tunnel into the forces of history by entering "the belly of the beast where new myths, new mass passions, and new mass movements are made." Bloom used simple correlational techniques plus what he calls "tuned empathy" and "saturated intuition" to help build or sustain the careers of figures like Prince, Michael Jackson,

Bob Marley, Bette Midler, Billy Joel, Paul Simon, Billy Idol, Peter Gabriel, David Byrne, John Mellencamp, Queen, Kiss, Aerosmith, AC/DC, Grandmaster Flash and The Furious Five, Run DMC, and roughly 100 others. In the process, he generated $28 billion in revenues (more than the gross domestic product of Oman or Luxembourg) for companies like Sony, Disney, Pepsi Cola, Coca Cola, and Warner Brothers.

Bloom also helped launch Farm Aid and Amnesty International's American presence. He worked with the United Negro College Fund,the National Black United Fund, and the NAACP, and he put together the first public service radio campaign for solar power (1981).

Bloom's focus on group behavior extends to geopolitics. He has debated one-one-one with senior officials from Egypt's Moslem Brotherhood and Gaza's Hamas on Iran's Arab-language international Alalam TV News Network. He has dissected headline issues on Saudi Arabia's KSA1-TV and on Iran's global English language Press-TV. And he has appeared fifty two times for up to five hours on 500 radio stations in North America.

Bloom is a former visiting scholar in the Graduate School of Psychology at NYU and a former core faculty member at the Graduate Institute in Meriden, Connecticut. In addition to arXiv.org, his scientific articles have appeared in PhysicaPlus, New Ideas in Psychology, and Across Species Comparisons and Psychopathology. Bloom has also written for The Washington Post, The Wall Street Journal, Wired, Knight-Ridder Financial News Service, the Village Voice, and Cosmopolitan. Bloom's 90-minute per episode YouTube series, Howard the Humongous, pulls in a minimum of 45,000 hits and a maximum of 161,000 per installment.

Topping it all off, Bloom's computer houses a not-so-secret and not-at-all humble project, his 7,100-chapter-long Grand Unified Theory of Everything in the Universe Including the Human Soul. Pavel Kurakin of the Keldysh Institute of Applied Mathematics of the Russian Academy of Sciences says that

"Bloom has created a new Scientific Paradigm. He explains in vast and compelling terms why we should forget all we know in

complicated modern math and should start from the very beginning. ...Bloom's Grand Unified Theory... opens a window into entire systems we don't yet know and/or see, new... collectivities that live, love, battle, win and lose each day of our gray lives. I never imagined that a new system of thought could produce so much light."

Concludes Joseph Chilton Pearce, author of Evolution's End and The Crack in the Cosmic Egg, "I have finished Howard Bloom's books, The Lucifer Principle and Global Brain, in that order, and am seriously awed, near overwhelmed by the magnitude of what he has done. I never expected to see, in any form, from any sector, such an accomplishment. I doubt there is a stronger intellect than Bloom's on the planet."

Nobel-Prize winner Dudley Herschbach calls Bloom's insights "truly awesome." There's a reason. Bloom's perspective comes from a once–in–the-history-of-science approach to the study of mass moods and cultural convolutions. Bloom started out normally enough, diving into microbiology, theoretical physics, and cosmology at the age of ten, building his first Boolean algebra machine at the age of twelve, becoming a dedicated microscopist that same year, codesigning a computer that won prizes at local science fairs before he left grade school, and being granted a private brainstorming session with the head of the Graduate Physics Department at the University of Buffalo when he was still twelve. By sixteen he was a lab assistant at the world's largest cancer research center, the Roswell Park Memorial Research Cancer Institute, where he helped plumb the mysteries of the immune system. And before his freshman year of college he designed and executed research in Skinnerian programmed learning at Rutgers University's Graduate School of Education.

(Continued On Page 55)

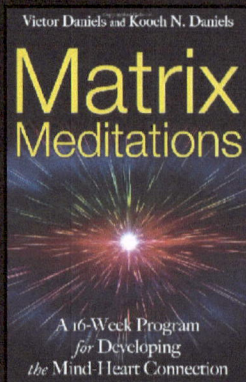

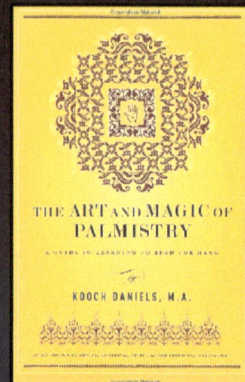

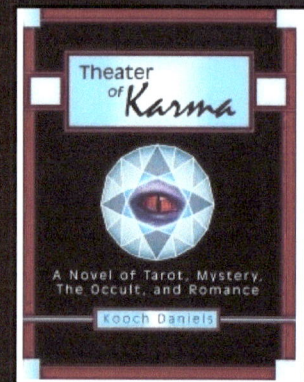

INSTANT EVOLUTION
The Influence of the City
on Human Genes
A Speculative Case
Continued From Page 53

Then came an act of academic heresy. After graduating magna cum laude and Phi Beta Kappa from New York University, Bloom turned down four graduate school fellowships and embarked on a 20-year-long urban anthropology expedition to penetrate what he calls "society's myth-making machinery"–the inner sanctums of politics and the media. During his foray into "the dark underbelly of mass emotion" he edited a magazine that won two National Academy of Poets prizes, founded the leading avant-garde art studio on the East Coast, was featured on the cover of Art Direction Magazine.

Then Bloom gave up listening to Beethoven, Bartok, and Mozart and entered a field he knew nothing about– he become editor of the rock monthly Circus. Using correlational studies, empirical surveys, ethnographic expeditions into suburban teen subcultures, and other scientific techniques, Bloom more than doubled Circus's sales, and was credited by Rolling Stones' Chet Flippo with founding a new genre–the heavy metal magazine. Seeking still further ways to infiltrate modernity's mass mind, Bloom founded the biggest public relations firm in the music industry, The Howard Bloom Organization, Ltd. The payoff in knowledge proved invaluable.

Bloom worked with Michael Jackson, Prince, John Cougar Mellencamp, Kiss, Queen, Bette Midler, Billy Joel, Joan Jett, Peter Gabriel, Diana Ross, Simon & Garfunkel, The Talking Heads, AC/DC, Billy Idol, Grandmaster Flash and the Furious Five, Run D.M.C., Simply Red, and the heads of many a media conglomerate. He was adept at spotting new subcultures, entering them, and helping their members crusade for the right to express their identity…a skill that gave him an inside role in the rise of country crossover, disco, midwestern rock, fusion jazz, New Age music, punk rock, rap, and the form of crossover black music embodied in Prince and Michael Jackson.

The pinnacles of fame provided surprising raw material for scientific analysis. "When you're at the center of the sort of attention-storm that hits when you're working with a superstar," Bloom says, "it's as if the laws of physics change. Hormones charge you up in ways you never imagined. Time perception alters. You resolve crises in minutes, seeing solutions instantly, solutions that previously would have taken you weeks.

"More important is the impact of a communal ritual like a rock concert. The star onstage is taken over by a self he doesn't know, one that seems to surge through him as if he were a length of empty pipe. The force of this strange passion welds the audience in an almost transcendent bond." Bloom's task was to first experience the exaltation, then to dissect it. "The model for this work," he says, "cames from William James, who attempted to feel the ecstatic experiences of mystics, then to probe these experieces scientifically, a process that led to his 1902 book The Varieties of the Religious Experience."

Bloom's forays into power and its manipulations were also intense. "In the music and film industry everyone knew that money and career advancement were on the line. But few realized how deeply what they did affected the lives of millions, and even fewer felt the responsibility that demands. It was an amazing privilege to work as an equal with the entertainment industry's elite, many of whom I either had to woo or thwart to help my clients reach their audience with a message of genuine value. Some executives were master strategists but used their intelligence to increase their own stature, often at a brutal cost to others. Others were far more ethical. Yet even the best-intentioned employed boardroom and backroom tactics handed down from the politics of chimpanzees. Without knowing it, they used tricks of leadership we share with social animals from lizards and lobsters to baboons and mountain apes."

The subculture of Washington politics was, to Bloom, the most disturbing of them all. Bloom co-founded Music in Action, a national anti-censorship organization. This brought him into head-on combat with Tipper Gore, wife of Vice President and eventual presidential candidate Al Gore. Says Bloom, "Tipper and the right wing religionists who used her for their ends were masters of perceptual manipulation. They perpetrated hoaxes of outrageous transparency, yet still managed to convince the press and public that their falsifications were true."

Twenty pages in The Billboard Guide to Music Publicity are devoted to Bloom and to the antidote he invented, "perceptual engineering," which he defines as "a way of finding a valid truth that the herd refuses to see, then turning the herd around and making that truth self-evident. It's what we do in much of science–seeing the ordinary from a new perspective, then revealing what makes it tick, and in the process altering society's views."

In 1981, Bloom organized the material he'd unearthed and began the formal research for a new theoretical structure that would first reveal itself in 1995's The Lucifer Principle: A Scientific Expedition Into the Forces of History. And he continued pursuing scientific truths in unconventional ways. In 1995 Bloom headed an insurgent academic circle called "The Group Selection Squad" whose efforts precipitated radical re-evaluations of neo-Darwinist dogma within the scientific community. In 1997, he founded a new discipline, paleopsychology, whose participants included physicists, psychologists, microbiologists, paleontologists, entomologists, neuroscientists, paleoneurologists, invertebrate zoologists, and systems theorists. Paleopsychology's mandate was to "map out the evolution of complexity, sociality, perception, and mentation from the first $10(-32)$ second of the Big Bang to the present."

Evolutionary biologist David Sloan Wilson has written that with his beyond-the-box insights Bloom has "raced ahead of the timid scientific herd" often "vaulting over their heads" with a "grand vision" that "we do strive as individuals, but we are also part of something larger than ourselves, with a complex physiology and mental life that we carry out but only dimly understand." In The Lucifer Principle, Global Brain, The Genius of the Beast, and his new book The God Problem: How A Godless Cosmos Creates, Howard Bloom brings those understandings from dimness into the light.

(Continued On Page 56)

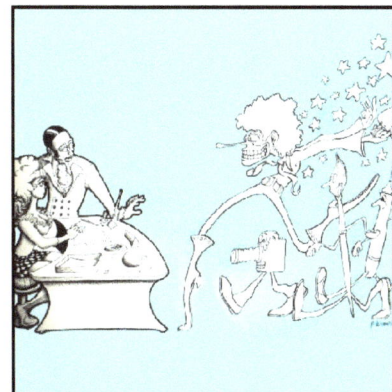

INSTANT EVOLUTION
The Influence of the City
on Human Genes
A Speculative Case
Continued From Page 55

ENDNOTES

[1] . Leda Cosmides and John Tooby. "Evolutionary Psychology: A Primer." Santa Barbara: Center for Evolutionary Psychology, University of California. http://www.clark.net/pub/ogas/evolution/EVPSYCH_primer.htm, downloaded June 1999.

[2] David P. Barash. The Whisperings Within: Evolution and the Origin of Human Nature. New York: Penguin Books, 1979.

[3] E.O. Wilson. Sociobiology: The New Synthesis. Cambridge: Harvard University Press, 1975.

[4] Barash also showed his serious side in an excellent textbook: David P. Barash. Sociobiology and Behavior . New York: Elsevier Scientific Publishing Company: 1977.

[5] David P. Barash. The Hare and The Tortoise: Culture, Biology, and Human Nature. New York: Viking, 1986.

[6] Nuclear Age Peace Foundation. "Countries with Nuclear Weapons Capability." http://www.wagingpeace.org/menu/issues/nuclear-weapons/index.htm , downloaded 5/2000.

[7] William K. Purves, Gordon H. Orians. Life: The Science of Biology. Sunderland, Massachusetts: Sinauer, 1987: 1032-1033.

[8] Jerome H. Barkow, Leda Cosmides, and John Tooby, editors . The Adapted Mind: Evolutionary Psychology and the Generation of Culture New York: Oxford University Press, 1992

[9] CNN/Time Interactive. "The Unabomber Case." http://www.cnn.com/US/9604/03/unabomber/index.html downloaed 5/2000.

[10] Tom Morton, producer and presenter. "The Descent of Man Episode 2: Stone Age Minds in Modern Skulls." Australian Broadcasting Corporation, 2000. http://www.abc.net.au/science/descent/trans2.htm, downloaded 5/2000.

[11] Says Neil Howell on his homepage, "We have hypothesized that the rate of mtDNA mutation is substantially higher than estimated previously with standard phylogenetic approaches. This hypothesis is being tested with an empirical approach that is free of assumptions and poorly controlled variables." (Neil Howell. "Genetics." The University of Texas Medical Branch at Galveston. downloaded 5/2000); Bruce Bower. "DNA's Evolutionary Dilemma." Science News, February 6, 1999: 89; M.W. Nachman, W.M. Brown, M. Stoneking, C.F. Aquadro. " Nonneutral mitochondrial DNA variation in humans and chimpanzees." Genetics, March 1996: 953-63.

[12] W.L Brown Jr. and E. O. Wilson. "Character Displacement." Systematic Zoology, 5 (2), 1956: 49-64; Edward O. Wilson. The Insect Societies: 454; Peter R. Grant. "Ecological character displacement." Science, 4 November 1994.

[13] D. Schluter. "Experimental Evidence that Competition Promotes Divergences in Adaptive Radiation." Science, 4 November 1994: 798. Ann Gibbons. "On the Many Origins of Species." Science, 13 September 1996: 1498.

[14] Lake Nyasa is also known as Lake Malawi.

[15] The traditional view, promoted by Ernst Mayr, is that groups need to be separated by a considerable distance to develop the genetic alterations that lead to speciation. However that model has proven to be incorrect, especially among fish. (Ernst Mayr. Populations, Species, and Evolution. Cambridge, MA: Harvard University Press, 1970; Tom Tregenza and Roger K. Butlin. "Speciation without isolation." Nature, 22 July 1999: 311-312; Virginia Morell. "Ecology Returns to Speciation Studies." Science, 25 June 1999: 2106-2108.)

[16] Virginia Morell. "Ecology Returns to Speciation Studies."

[17] C. Sturmbauer, A. Meyer. "Genetic divergence, speciation and morphological stasis in a lineage of African cichlid fishes." Nature, August 13, 1992: 578; Malcolm T. Smith and Robert Layton. "Still Human After All These Years." The Sciences, January-February 1989: 10; Ole Seehausen, Jacques J.M. van Alphen, Frans Witte. "Cichlid Fish Diversity Threatened by Eutrophication That Curbs Sexual Selection." Science, 19 September 1997: 1808-1810.

[18] K. Byrne, R.A. Nichols . "Culex pipiens in London Underground tunnels: differentiation between surface and subterranean populations. " Heredity , January 1999 (Pt 1): 7-15 .

[19] Agence France-Presse. " Report claims London Underground home to new species of mosquito." http://en.wikipedia.org/wiki/London_Underground_mosquito

[20] Sherrie L. Lyons, "The Origins of T.H. Huxley's Saltationism: History in Darwin's Shadow," Journal of the History of Biology 28, 1995: 463-494.

[21] . Scott P. Carroll, Hugh Dingle, Stephen P. Klassen. "Genetic differentiation of fitness-associated traits among rapidly evolving populations of soapberry bug." Evolution, 51 (4), 1997: 1182-1188. Kelly Kissane, University of Maryland, personal communication, May 15, 1998.

[22] J.B. Losos, K.I. Warheit, T.W. Schoener . "Adaptive differentiation following experimental island colonization in Anolis lizards." Nature 1997 387:70-73. The St. Louis: Losos Lab, Washington University. http://www.biology.wustl.edu/~lososlab/nature97.html, downloaded 5/2000.

[23] John N. Thompson. "The Evolution of Species Interactions." Science, 25 June 1999: 2116-2118.

[24] John N. Thompson. "The Evolution of Species Interactions": 2116-2118.

[25] Ann Gibbons. "Archaeologists Rediscover Cannibals." Science, 1 August 1997: 635-637.

[26] Ann Gibbons. "Archaeologists Rediscover Cannibals": 635-637.

[27] Alban Defleur, Tim White, Patricia Valensi, Ludovic Slimak, & Evelyne Crégut-Bonnoure . " Neanderthal Cannibalism at Moula-Guercy, Ardeche, France. " Science, 1 Oct 1999: 128 – 131.

[28] Hartmut Thieme. "Lower Paleolithic hunting spears from Germany," Nature, 27 February 1997: 807-810

[29] Valerius Geist believes strongly that teeth were among the weapons humans used to attack each other until fairly recent times. See his Life Strategies. , Human Evolution, Environmental Design: Toward a Biological Theory of Health . New York: Springer-Verlag, 1978.

[32] Kathleen M. Kenyon. "Excavations at Jericho, 1957-58." Palestine Excavation Quarterly, 92, 1960: 88-108; Purushottam Singh. Neolithic Cultures of Western Asia. New York: Seminar Press, 1974: 33-47; David Ussishkin. "Notes on the Fortifications of the Middle Bronze II Period at Jericho and Shechem." Bulletin of the American Schools of Oriental Research, November, 1989.

[33] James Mellaart. Catal-Huyuk: A Neolithic Town in Anatolia. New York: McGraw-Hill, 1967.

[34] Jack R. Harlan. The Living Fields: Our Agricultural Heritage. New York: Cambridge University Press, 1995. http://wcb.ucr.edu/wcb/schools/CNAS/bpsc/agomezpo/1/modules/page42.html, downloaded 5/2000.

[35] Keith Thomas. Man and the Natural World: A History of The Modern Sensibility. New York: Pantheon Books, 1983.

[36] Klint Baggett. "The Neolithic Revolution and the De-evolution of Health." Tuscaloosa, AL: Department of Anthropology, The University of Alabama, March 3, 1999. http://www.as.ua.edu/ant/bindon/ant475/Papers/baggett2.html, downloaded 5/2000. Because this paper sums up a standardized point of view so nicely, let me quote from it at length: "Perhaps no other event has had a greater impact on humanity's health than the so called Neolithic Revolution. This gradual shift to cultivation occurred at different times for different places, usually between 5,000 and 10,000 years BP (Larsen 1984). Even today man has to always find ways to maximize his crop yield in order to keep up with the ever growing population. For hundreds of thousands of years man had been a nomadic hunter and gatherer. His diet, laden with protein and energy rich foods had enabled him to survive and to evolve into a healthy, lean form. By the end of the last ice age man had moved into every inhabitable part of the planet (Kiple 1997). It was perhaps the decline of resources coupled with the growing population that prompted some peoples to start cultivating primary food sources. Most infectious diseases can now be traced back to this time when man first began to aggregate in large numbers (McKeown 1976). We must remember that for essentially all of our existence as humans, hunting and gathering had been our mode of subsistence (Armelagos and McArdle, 1975). The fact that our genetic makeup had adapted to this way of life would have drastic consequences when man shifted to more of a horticultural subsistence (Relethford 1994). Recent archaeological evidence sheds light on the possibility that the Neolithic Revolution may have been a backwards tumble in our evolution...." On the other side of the issue, several studies have recently questioned the idea that hunters and gatherers were splendidly nourished as sheer romantic distortion. See: Suzanne Austin Alchon. "The Great Killers in Precolumbian America: A Hemispheric Perspective." Latin American Population History Bulletin. Number 27, Fall 1997. Department of History, University of Minnesota, Posted December 30, 1997. http://www.hist.umn.edu/~rmccaa/laphb/27fall97/laphb27a.htm, downloaded 5/2000; Mark L. Wahlqvist. "Critical nutrition events in human history." Asia Pacific Journal of Clinical Nutrition, n. 1, 1992: 101-105.

[30] Arther Ferrill "Neolithic Warfare– The Second-Oldest Profession.." MHQ: The Quarterly Journal of Military History. Fall 1990 v 3 n 1. http://eng.hss.cmu.edu/history/neolithic-war.txt, downloaded May 2000.

[31] Allen W. Johnson and Timothy Earle. The Evolution of Human Societies: From Foraging Group to Agrarian State. Stanford: Stanford University Press, 1987: 56.

[37] McGuire Gibson. "Population shift and the rise of Mesopotamian civilisation." In The organisation of culture change: models in prehistory, edited by Colin Renfrew. Pittsburgh: University of Pittsburgh Press, 1973: 448-450.

[38] Howard Bloom. The Lucifer Principle: a scientific expedition into the forces of history. New York: Atlantic Monthly Press, 1995.

[39] Victor Mendoza Grado, Ricardo Salvador . "What Is The Indian Population of Mexico?" Culture and Society of Mexico, http://www.public.iastate.edu/~rjsalvad/scmfaq/indpop.html, downloaded 5/2000.

(Continued On Page 57)

INSTANT EVOLUTION
The Influence of the City on Human Genes
A Speculative Case
Continued From Page 56

[40] Shirley C. Strum. Almost Human: A Journey into the World of Baboons. New York: Random House, 1987: 173-183, 205, 249.

[41] Suzanne Austin Alchon. "The Great Killers in Precolumbian America, A Hemispheric Perspective."

[42] "... the most important of all causes of organic change is one which is almost independent of altered and perhaps suddenly altered physical conditions, namely, the mutual relation of organism to organism...." Charles Darwin.

On the Origin of Species by Means of Natural Selection, or The Preservation of Favoured Races in the Struggle for Life. In Library of the Future, 4th Edition, Ver. 5.0. Irvine, CA: World Library, Inc., 1996. CD-Rom.

[43] . Heather Pringle. "Death in Norse Greenland." Science, 14 February 1997: 924-926; J.P. Mallory. In Search of the Indo-Europeans: Language, Archaeology, and Myth. New York: Thames and Hudson, 1989.

[44] . Manuel de Landa. A Thousand Years of Nonlinear History. New York: Zone Books, 1997: 142. William H. Durham. Coevolution: Genes, Culture, and Human Diversity. Stanford, CA: Stanford University Press, 1991: 283.

[45] . For a review of many post agricultural and post-urban genetic adaptations in humans, including those involving such basics as skull shape and the configuration of teeth, see: Valerius Geist. Life Strategies, Human Evolution, Environmental Design: Toward a Biological Theory of Health: 388-401.

[46] William K. Purves, Gordon H. Orians. Life: The Science of Biology. Sunderland, Massachusetts: Sinauer, 1987: 1034.

[47] . S.L. Wiesenfeld. "Sickle-cell trait in human biological and cultural evolution. Development of agriculture causing increased malaria is bound to gene-pool changes causing malaria reduction." Science, 8 September 1967: 1134-1140. Several groups of genetic researchers have attempted to establish a far older date for the evolution of sickle-cell anemia. However even Stine, et. al., who champion an ancient origin for the sickle-cell gene, acknowledge that its appearance is "usually attributed to recent...mutations." (O.C. Stine, G.J. Dover, D. Zhu, K.D. Smith. "The evolution of two west African populations." Journal of Molecular Evolution, April 1992: 336-44.)

[48] Measles is caused by a close relative of the rinderpest-producing paramyxovirus (genus Morbillivirus). A second close relation of the paramyxovirus appears in another post-domestication-era human companion: the dog. Here it manifests itself as distemper.

[49] We tend to think of measles as a relatively harmless disease of childhood. However measles produces a sub-illness (subacute sclerosing panencephalitis) which attacks the nervous system, leading to a deterioration of mental abilities, a loss of control of the body's muscles, and a crumbling of the ability to speak. This state ends six to nine months later in blindness, dementia, stupor, and death.

[50] William H. McNeill. Plagues and Peoples. New York: Anchor Books, 1998 (original edition 1976): 208-224; Jared Diamond. Guns, Germs, and Steel: the Fates of Human Societies. New York: W.W. Norton, 1997; Manuel De Landa. A Thousand Years of Nonlinear History: 132-133.

[51] Mary Douglas. Natural Symbols: Explorations in Cosmology. New York: Pantheon Books, 1982.

[52] Mark Pluciennik. "A perilous but necessary search: archaeology and European identities." Lampeter: Department of Archaeology, University of Wales. http://65.54.113.26/Author/34420159/mark-pluciennik. []

The MOHAMMAD CODE
Why A Desert Prophet Wants You Dead

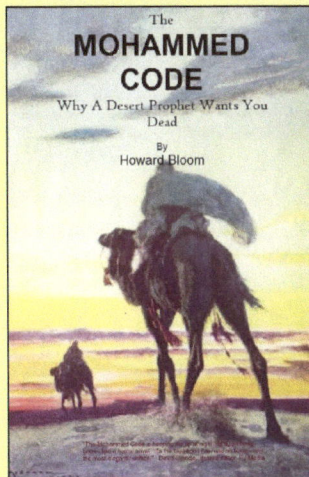

By Howard Bloom

"The Mohammed Code is keeping me up at night. It's a terrifying book—like a horror novel. It's the best book I've read on Islam...and the most elegantly written." David Swindle, lifestyle editor, PJ Media

Alexander the Great, Julius Caesar, Napoleon, and Adolph Hitler tried to take over the world. All of them failed. Yet an illiterate desert prophet enabled his followers to hammer together an empire 11 times the size of Alexander the Great's conquests, 5 times the size of the Roman Empire, and 7 times the size of the USA. How did Mohammed pull it off? And how does his success threaten you and me?

The Mohammed Code is a story you are not supposed to read.

The Mohammed Code is based entirely on Islamic sources: the Quran, the Hadith, Ibn Ishaq, al Tabari, and lives of Mohammed written for Moslem eyes only by Islamic religious leaders, Islamic scholars, and Islamic journalists. The Mohammed Code tells one of the most important and riveting stories in history. The hidden story behind the headlines from shock-spots in Asia, Africa, Europe, Iran, Iraq, Afghanistan, and Pakistan. And the inner secrets of the mosque down the street.

If you are a Moslem and you want to be righteous, just, and pure, you are required to follow in the footsteps of Mohammed. What kind of footsteps did Mohammed leave you? His example as the commander of 65 military campaigns. His example as a participant in 27 of those battles. His example as the architect of ethnic expulsions and genocides.

Explains Osama bin Laden, Mohammed was "a Prophet of Conquest." And Pakistan's Universal Sunnah Foundation agrees. It says proudly that under Mohammed's generalship, "Islam spread on an average of 822 square kilometres per day." Behind that conquest is an astonishing story.

The story of Mohammed's life as a militant. The story of Mohammed's two favorite tools of war, "deceit" (deception) and "terror." The story that led to the assembly of the biggest empire in human history...an empire eleven times the size of the conquests of Alexander the Great, five times the size of the Roman Empire, and seven times the size of the United States.

The Mohammed Code is the story of how Mohammed laid out a simple goal--seizing the entire world. A goal so dependent on violence that one of Mohammed's leading modern interpreters, Islamic Revolutionary Iran's founding father, the Ayatollah Khomeini, says proudly that "Islam has obliterated many tribes." The Mohammed Code tells a story unknown in the West, the story that led the Ayatollah to declare that, "Moslems have no alternative... to an armed holy war. ...Holy war means the conquest of all non Moslem territories. ...It will ...be the duty of every able-bodied adult male to volunteer for this war of conquest, the final aim of which is to put Koranic law in power from one end of the earth to the other."

If you want to know the story of Mohammed's ten years as a militant, read The Mohammed Code. It is more than just amazing. It is a story whose aftershocks are quaking your life.

www.HowardBloom.net

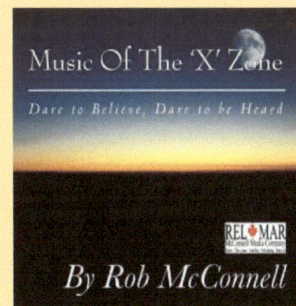

Could Body Cams Reduce Police Tensions?
Discovery News

If Ferguson, Mo. police officer Darren Wilson had been wearing a camera when 18-year-old Michael Brown was killed last week, the details of the case would almost assuredly be indisputable.

But the effort to lesson unnecessary police force may not be as simple as slapping a body cam on every officer in the country.

"There have been a lot of claims in favor and against [body cameras], and there are only five studies in the entire body of literature on the subject," said Michael White, an associate professor in the School of Criminology and Criminal Justice at Arizona State University, who recently concluded in a report for the U.S. Department of Justice that there is not enough evidence to make a recommendation for or against them.

"There's enough evidence that if a department is interested they should proceed, but with caution," he said.

Currently more than 1,000 U.S. police departments are equipping officers with body cameras. The cameras are a step beyond police patrol car dashboard cameras, whose footage have helped piece together incidents for decades.

In the Ferguson case, White thinks police body cams could have helped ease tensions.

"In cases like we're seeing in Ferguson, we're hearing two very, very different versions of events. If he had worn a camera they could have gone to the video, and the potential would have been for it not to escalate: if the bystanders view was accurate and it was murder, then they could have proceeded with the firing and arresting and prosecuting of the officer. Or if the flip side were true, then work could have been done with the community stakeholders to explain what happened step by step."

The details can be both complex and cumbersome, however: Officers and unions -- who may be reluctant to adapt the technology -- must be on board with a mandate. And even something as seemingly simple as storing the data becomes prohibitive when deployed on such a massive scale. Then there are bigger issues, such as privacy."The same technology that lets us do these things can also be abused," said Dan Gillmor, who teaches digital media literacy at Arizona State University. "I think we all deserve a zone of privacy in our normal lives, and these devices we carry around are just dandy as surveillance on us. But there's a growing belief that for people who have life and death power over others, it's quite proper for them to have ongoing recordings of their interactions with the public."

The ideal scenario, White said, would be for police departments to garner support from the ground up: involve officers, unions, and the community in decision-making, and address privacy concerns and resources up front, he suggests.

With the recent controversy still simmering in Ferguson, Missouri, Trace examines the use of lethal force by police officers.

Of course, it's not only police officers who can record a crime. In fact, most police chiefs advise officers to assume that everything they're doing is being recorded.

"It's a sad comment on the state of law enforcement, but I now encourage people who see the police doing something that seems out of the ordinary to document it with pictures or video and save it (if not post it online)," wrote Dan Gillmor,in The Guardian.

But even those who espouse citizen involvement, such as the American Civil Liberties Union, are rooting for police cameras.

"The use of cameras to document the abuse of power is an important development," Gillmor said. "But the ideal thing would've been for the police themselves to be wearing cameras."

The public seems to agree: Two online citizen petitions calling for police to wear cameras have garnered over 150,000 signatures.

And despite his inconclusive research, White predicts that police body cameras may follow the same trajectory as Tasers, which became common in police departments within a span of a decade.

"This technology has the potential to expand that quickly if all the concerns are addressed," he said.

The price of the cameras have dropped substantially in the last 18 months, White said, and last week, Taser stock prices increased 10 percent, which most attribute to demand for its body cameras. []

Smile! Police to Wear Live-Action Body Cameras
Discovery News

Police officers across London will wear video cameras when responding to emergency calls as part of a year-long pilot project launched on Thursday. A total of 500 cameras will routinely collect evidence from public order and domestic abuse incidents in 10 of London's 32 boroughs, as well as potentially contentious "stop and searches," Scotland Yard said.

The force has been testing body-worn cameras for several years but was given new impetus following the police shooting of suspected gang member Mark Duggan in 2011, which sparked days of rioting in the capital and cities across England.

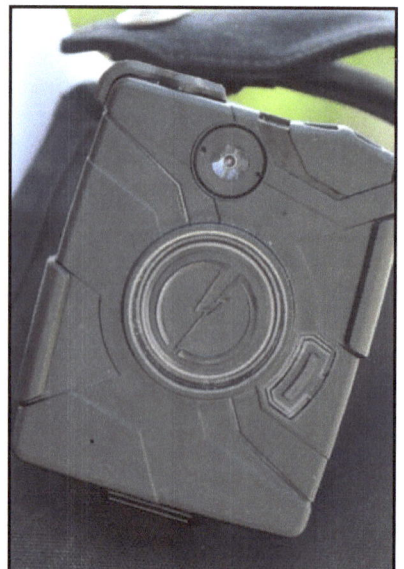

An inquest jury in January found the killing was lawful but the coroner noted the "stark problem" posed by contradictions between the notes from officers at the scene and mobile phone video evidence taken by witnesses. Scotland Yard Commissioner Hogan-Howe said at the time that armed police would in future wear video cameras to ensure a more accurate record was made of their actions.

The police chief said Thursday that the cameras, being trialled by unarmed officers, could also deter people from becoming violent towards police and speed up justice by providing a compelling reason for criminals to plead guilty.

"I believe it will also show our officers at their best, dealing with difficult and dangerous situations every day but it will also provide clearer evidence when it's been alleged that we got things wrong," he said. "That has to be in both our own and the public's interest."

The data from the cameras will be uploaded at the end of every officer's shift and kept on file for a month before being deleted, unless it is required as evidence.

The cameras will not be permanently switched on and officers, who will wear them on their stab vests, have been told to alert members of the public "as soon as practical" that they are being recorded. Failure to switch on the cameras as directed in police guidance will be treated as a disciplinary offense, Hogan-Howe said. []

The Psychology of Alien Abduction: An Altered State of Consciousness?

by
Dr. Emile Gurstelle

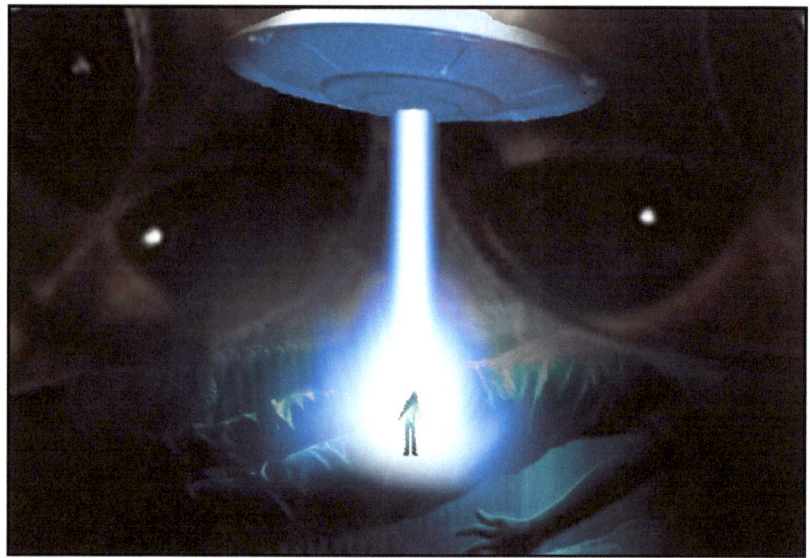

poiler Alert! If you are convinced you were abducted by aliens, please do not read any further. I have neither the desire nor the ability to change your belief. That said, the research shows that the event perceived as an "alien abduction" is an altered state of consciousness. The belief that one has been kidnapped by extraterrestrials is not.

I just finished reading an engrossing study called Abducted: How People Come to Believe They Were Kidnapped by Aliens by Susan A. Clancy, PhD, published by Harvard University Press. Dr. Clancy, a post doctoral fellow in psychology at Harvard, was doing research with people with "recovered" memories of childhood sexual abuse. She became frustrated because there was no way to know with certainty whether these people recovered memories of actual abuse or factitious events. She decided to "repeat the study with a population that I could be sure had 'recovered' false memories. Alien abductions seemed to fit the bill. (p. 20)"

Dr. Clancy interviewed and conducted laboratory memory studies of over fifty volunteers who sincerely believed they were abducted. Her sense was that these people were not lying. Only one of her participants was psychotic. The rest were normally functioning people, most of who felt that the abduction experience, though harrowing, changed their lives for the better. The group included a physician, a librarian, a veteran, an MBA, a chef, a fitness instructor, a construction worker, Ivy Leaguers, geeks, housewives, teenagers, grandfathers and school teachers.

About the only personality characteristic the sample group had in common was schizotypy. People with schizotypy are more likely than others to be perceived as eccentrics, engage in magical thinking and experience perceptual distortions. For example, one might "sense" the presence of another person. They tend to interpret incidents and events as having a special and unusual meaning. They may be prone toward a belief in superstitions. While people with schizotypy are not psychotic, they have a greater likelihood than the general population to have close relatives with schizophrenia. Clancy concludes that "these people are not crazy. They tend to have unusual ideas, experiences, and beliefs – ones that don't necessarily conform to mainstream social

beliefs and tendencies. They believe not only in alien abduction, but also in things like ESP, astrology, tarot, channeling, auras, holistic medicine, and crystal therapy. (p. 134)"

So, how do people wind up believing they were abducted by aliens? The belief usually begins with an altered state of consciousness. In earlier posts I described a variation of hypnagogia that I suggested could occur during waking hours. However, standard hypnagogia refers to hallucinatory or quasi-hallucinatory events that occur in the process of falling asleep or upon awakening. During certain sleep cycles our bodies are immobilized by the nervous system so that we aren't acting out our dreams. This is called sleep paralysis. If we wake up while we are still dreaming, the paralysis may persist into the waking state along with hypnagogic remnants of the dream including hallucinations of sights, sounds and tactile sensations. It can take up to a half a minute for our sleep – wake cycles to resynchronize and for the sleep paralysis and dream-like material to fade. As with any other hallucination, the sensations may seem very real. Most of us chalk these normal experiences up to what they actually are, but those who are so inclined may attach special meanings to such events.

Since the advent of science fiction movies of invaders from outer space, people who report abductions tend to tell the same general story:

An unsuspecting ordinary human gets kidnapped by extraterrestrial beings for medical examination or sexual experimentation... Both the details [big heads, wrap-around eyes, reversible amnesia, and probing needles] and the general plot existed n the movies and on TV before people ever reported personal knowledge of them...Alien abduction reports... began only after they were featured on TV and in the movies. (Clancy, p. 83)

Now, not all believers in alien abduction initially interpret the hypnagogic sleep paralysis as an extraterrestrial kidnapping for medical or sexual purposes. Rather, they sense something is wrong with them. Perhaps they have unexplained physical and mental ailments, such as strange marks, pain, changes in sexual

functioning or panic attacks. Believing that alien abduction could be possible, they seek the services of a hypnotist to try to find out the cause of their symptoms. It has already been documented that hypnotic trance can unintentionally produce false recovered memories of childhood sexual abuse. Thus, a hypnotist working with some people may unwittingly guide them into developing "memories" of an alien abduction. These "recovered" memories seem as real as memories of an actual event. Similar false memories have also been created in the laboratory.

Another complication reinforcing the belief in abduction in most of Clancy's participants was the perception that the abduction was a "transformative [life] event." Abductees reported that these experiences provided meaning in their lives, gave them wisdom, enlarged their word view or expanded their realities. "For many people, belief in alien abduction gratifies spiritual hungers.(p. 150)" "Not surprisingly," according to Clancy, "once you 'discover' your place in the universe, you have a hard time being a skeptic. (p. 149)."

In essence, the people most likely to believe they were abducted by aliens are those who are predisposed to favor paranormal over scientific explanations. Without conscious awareness they apply their interest in and exposure to stories of extraterrestrials to provide a complex explanation to what most people accept as a normal altered state of consciousness. They often have physical and/or emotional symptoms for which they don't seek common explanations. Some may "recover" memories of being abducted through hypnosis or other forms of guided imagery. The belief in abduction then tends to become sealed in stone when it fills an otherwise spiritual void.

About The Author:

Dr. Gurstelle, Ph.D is a licensed clinical psychologist in Butler, NJ and is director of Wayne Psychological Group, LLC. He is a former assistant professor at William Paterson University in Wayne, NJ. His special interests are in the psychology of consciousness, psychological well-being of children, anxiety disorders and coping with trauma. []

Understanding The Psychology Of Ghosts

By J Allan Danelek

In this part, we will examine some of the more common reasons paranormal investigators give to explain why some spirits seem to prefer to stay earthbound while others appear to move on effortlessly. As such, this section will, in many ways, have far more to do with psychology than parapsychology as we examine the ghostly psyche and see if we can figure out what might make a person decide to haunt his old neighborhood when it could well be doing more interesting things with its time. In effect, we will be doing nothing less than exploring the question of what makes a ghost 'tick', which usually makes for lively debate.

While at first glance this attempt to understand the ghostly psyche would appear to be beyond our ability to hypothesize, I disagree. A ghost is only human after all, and we do know a few things about human behavior that we might transpose onto our ethereal colleagues in an attempt to better understand them. Ghostly behavior, after all, shouldn't really be all that different from normal human behavior, even if the consciousness that powers it exists within another context of reality. Hopefully, that should be enough to help us answer many of our basic questions.

Ghost By Choice or By Accident?

Perhaps the first thing we need to do it try and determine what factors go into deciding whether a particular person is likely to become a ghost. For example, does becoming a ghost happen to everyone when they die or only to some? Is it something we choose to do, or can we be trapped on the earth plane and be impelled to roam the world of the living for all eternity? Obviously, we can't know the answers to these questions with anything approaching certainty, but there are some guidelines we might use.

The first thing to understand about a ghost—and I'm limiting the discussion here purely to those entities we've previously identified as personalities (human based ghosts)—is that where human beings are concerned, not even death can change things. I believe that when a person dies, they move onto the next realm with all the personality traits, quirks, prejudices, biases, and a lifetime of accumulated wisdom—and nonsense—fully intact. Working from that premise, then, it's not difficult to imagine how some people would either choose to become a ghost or might find

themselves trapped on the physical plane by their own personality flaws. As such, we might assume that the reasons for becoming a ghost may be as numerous and varied as are the types of personalities humans exhibit. Let's look at just a few of the more prevalent ghost types and explore their possible rationale for choosing to remain in the physical realm:

GHOST "TYPES"

- The Unaware Ghost
- The Denial Ghost
- The Attached Ghost
- The Jealous Ghost
- The Fearful Ghost
- The Melancholy or Sad Ghost
- The Mission Ghost
- The Goodbye or Comfort Ghost
- The Curious Ghost
- The Mischievous Ghost
- The Angry Ghost

The Unaware Ghost:

Many paranormal investigators believe that some entities may remain within the physical realm simply because they are not aware that they are dead. As such, they go on about their life much as they did before completely oblivious to the fact that they are no longer a part of the physical realm and remain that way until some sudden trauma or realization goads them into either remembering that they have died or demonstrates that they are, in fact, no longer among the living. This idea has been popularized by such excellent movies as The Sixth Sense and The Others and is a part of many people's beliefs about ghosts (a perception Hollywood has done much to reinforce.)

I, however, find it extremely unlikely that ghosts don't know they're dead. Near Death Experience (NDE) accounts remain remarkably consistent in their insistence that even upon sudden and unexpected death the soul

invariably detaches from the body and hovers about nearby, all the while aware of its surroundings and cognizant of the fact that it is no longer attached to its physical body. If these accounts are accurate portrayals of what the human psyche experiences at the moment of death, it seems that to not be aware of the fact that one had 'passed over' would be about as hard to miss as would be the loss of a limb; some things, it seems, are just a little too obvious not to notice. Unless one died in their sleep or was so inebriated when they passed that they never knew what hit them, I should imagine the one thing we could not help but notice is our own death, especially once one started encountering deceased loved ones and, perhaps, various religious figures. As such, I seriously doubt that any recently deceased spirit would be in-or, at least, remain in-a state of ignorance long. It simply doesn't hold together logically.

That being said, however, it is possible that children or the mentally incapacitated might not recognize the situation for what it is and remain attached to the physical plane after their death. Ghosts of children are frequent subjects of a haunting, leading to the possibility that children who are unable to comprehend death in practical terms may well be too confused to move on after their demise. Death is, after all, generally considered a 'grown up' affair that is rarely discussed with children. As such, some may have no real understanding of what is happening to them and so remain trapped in a type of 'sleep state' until they either can finally comprehend what has happened and move on or are rescued by other spiritual entities whose job it is to look out for these gentle souls and guide them along.

(Continued On Page 62)

Understanding The Psychology Of Ghosts
Continued From Page 61

Such an entity would be more akin to an 'immature' or 'childish' ghost than to an 'unaware' ghost however, though, of course, such distinctions are probably more a matter of semantics. For the most part, however, it is probably safe to assume that most humans will recognize when they are dead and leave it at that.

The Denial Ghost:

While it is unlikely that a mature and psychologically stable person would be unaware that they have died, it is entirely plausible that there could be those who find the idea so traumatic that they refuse to accept the fact and live on in utter denial of their new reality. While at first thought this idea may sound preposterous, it is not so hard to accept when one considers that just as there are people who make denial a major part of their life, it is only natural to imagine that there are those personalities who will make it an integral part of their afterlife as well and so will simply refuse to accept the truth of their own Earthly demise. Denial, after all, seems to be such a big part of what it is to be a human in the first place that I can't imagine it wouldn't remain a big part of some people's identity after death as well-at least in some cases.

Of course, denying one's death may sound very similar to being unaware of it, but there is a big difference. The unaware ghost allegedly doesn't realize it is dead whereas even the most obstinate denial ghost knows, at least on some level, that it is dead and is simply refusing to acknowledge the fact. After all, that's the whole point of denial; it is only necessary when one is aware that there is a truth that needs to be suppressed.

Now how this might work is a source of some debate. Some personalities may simply choose to go on as if nothing has happened and ignore every obvious sign that they no longer exist within a physical context in the process. This is possibly what happens to many historical personalities who refuse to vacate a particular location; they won't leave because they can't bear the idea they might be dead and so they remain, going about their day-to-day affairs as if nothing has changed. They are like the elderly Hollywood starlet who bemoans the lack of privacy her fame has brought long after her name has been forgotten, and refuses to open the door in any case because a part of her knows the adoring throngs of fans she so disdains will not be there. As such, they can be the ones who remain earthbound the longest, for human pride can be as powerful and debilitating on the other side as it often proves to be on this side of eternity, which can make it especially difficult to convince them to give up the charade and move on.

The Attached Ghost:

Though in many ways similar to the denial ghost, this type of ghost knows and even fully acknowledges that it is dead, but is so emotionally attached to the things of the world that it refuses to let go of them. This is often their home or some place they truly loved, resulting in their energy being too enmeshed within the physical realm-their emotions and perceptions still too 'earth heavy'-for them to move on (or, for that matter, even begin to explore their new dimensions of existence.) And so they stay behind, always hovering on the edge of human perception but rarely if ever able to interact with it in any meaningful way. To many of these entities then, death is seen simply as a tremendous impediment in their enjoyment of life that they do their best to ignore or work around.

Such ghosts also often remain around for years or even decades, so great is their attachment to the things of the world. Even if they can no longer enjoy the things they own or even be able to interact with their loved ones, it is still better than not having them at all (or so it might be reasoned from their perspective.) They tend to be the more possessive ghosts who insist that new residents leave their home or attempt to interfere in the lives of those they left behind, sometimes in rather significant ways. If strong willed enough, such entities may stay a very long time, usually not leaving until either their home has been bulldozed or so dramatically altered as to make it 'unlivable' to them. Only then may such ghosts begin to fade and dissipate, though it may be some time before they finally are willing to concede the futility of remaining behind and move on.

As such, people of a possessive or sentimental nature who are extremely attached to the world, or who are otherwise incapable of functioning outside of the familiar walls of the tiny world they have created for themselves are good subjects for becoming an attached ghost. Over-identification with one's profession or trade can also produce this effect (ghosts of librarians or school janitors, for instance, are examples of this) and elderly couples and shut-ins who have learned to isolate themselves from the outside world especially run this risk, and so need to consider the potential repercussions their self-imposed exile may have in the next world if they are not careful. It is never helpful to attach great importance to anything in the physical realm, for it is a temporal environment that is constantly in a state of flux and beyond anyone's ability to control. Attached ghosts are simply those individuals who have yet to realize that fact.

The Jealous Ghost:

Though exceedingly rare, there are accounts of ghostly entities attaching themselves not to things, but to people, and interjecting themselves into earthly relationships, usually out of some misguided notion of possessiveness or outright jealousy. This could be anything from an over-possessive spouse that can't accept the thought of their mate remarrying to a spurned lover who took his or her own life only to come back and attach themselves to the source of their unrequited affections later. Active only around the source of their possessiveness and then usually only when in the presence of that source's newfound affections, the jealous ghost can be among the most difficult, frightening and hard to get along with of all.

However, while this type of ghost is very similar to the attached ghost in that it refuses to break its earthly links because of something in the physical realm it has over identified with, its source of attention is so limited and fixed that it can usually be gotten rid of fairly easily. Once the still living partner remarries (or otherwise makes it abundantly clear to the interfering entity that they intend to get on with their life) it will usually dissipate and move on to other pursuits (though not without usually loitering for a while longer just in case the source of their affection changes their mind.) In some cases, however, it is only the death of its partner that finally ends the haunting, meaning that if it is obstinate enough, a jealous ghost could end up hanging around for decades (though this would be unlikely.)

As such, overly jealous, possessive, or controlling individuals need to be especially careful they don't end up stuck on the physical plane after they die because of their stubborn unwillingness to give up that which they don't truly own in any case. It takes very little, it seems, to stay attached to the temporal realm, so one would be wise to do some introspection where relationships are concerned to see if they may be a good candidate to become a jealous ghost, and what changes they might need to make in their life to avoid that fate.

The Fearful Ghost:

Due to cultural or religious conditioning, some personalities are simply too afraid to find out what fate has in store for them and so prefer the mundane existence of a haunting to the potential punishment a final judgment might portend. Often these are individuals who did considerable harm-or believe they did-to others and so fear being called out for their offenses and punished. To them, then, remaining within the comparative safety of the physical realm is their only means of avoiding this judgment and the punishment they believe they so richly deserve, and so they cling to the material world the way a frightened child might cling to it's mother's leg on the first day of school. In essence, then, fearful ghosts are doing nothing less than hiding from Hell.

It's not just evil doers who find themselves in this state, however, but ordinary people who have been subjected to various fundamentalist religious teachings from childhood—teachings they are certain they have failed to live up to—and so retain a fear of being eternally punished for 'backsliding' or for committing some other real or imagined transgression. Guilt and shame can be powerful fear inducers for some people, especially among those who have grown up in a background of religious intolerance or maintained firmly held beliefs in such things as divine wrath, original sin, eternal retribution, judgment, and the reality of hell.

(Continued On Page 63)

Understanding The Psychology Of Ghosts
Continued From Page 62

As such, then, people who have had strong religious beliefs drilled into them from childhood and feel they have not lived up to them are good candidates to become fearful ghosts, especially if they believe God is angry with them and they have not had a chance to 'repent' or had their sins absolved by a priest before they died. Fear is almost as strong an emotion as love, and can keep one tied to the earth plane as completely as denial, possessiveness, and jealousy can, and is easily capable of making us our own worst enemy and more adroit at inadvertently torturing ourselves than any external foe—or Deity—could ever be.

The Melancholy or Sad Ghost:

The fact that some people are so overwhelmed by grief to the point of incapacitation is a sad reminder of the power of unresolved loss to hold a human soul in limbo long after the body that housed that soul has died. As such, we shouldn't be surprised when this type of negative energy manages to manifest itself without our physical realm in the form of the 'sad' or 'melancholy' ghost.

Perhaps the most depressing type of entity one can encounter, the 'sad' ghost is someone who is so overwhelmed by some tragedy that they continue to wander the physical realm as if in a state of shock that they seem unable to recover from. Suicides often end up as 'sad' ghosts, for the same factors that drove them to take their own life frequently keep them bound to the very physical realm they took such pains to rid themselves of. As such, they can also be among the most difficult to 'rescue', for they are often too self-absorbed in their own pain to either recognize the need for salvation or care about it. They truly are the most lost of all souls, and may require significant intervention on both the part of the living and other spiritual entities to pull them towards the light.

Melancholy ghosts often announce their presence by filling a room with an air of sadness or despair that can dramatically impact the still living in often profound ways. They may also be the source of many cemetery hauntings, for in their grief at their loss of life and happiness, they may be drawn to the physical remains of what had once been their only earthly source of joy. In essence, a 'sad' ghost may be drawn to the physical remains of themselves or a loved one in the same way a grieving mother is to the casket of her child. They simply cannot let go of their loss long enough to even notice their own unfortunate state, and so remain walking a never ending treadmill of pain, regret and despair.

As such, people who suffer from chronic depression or are suicidal need to be aware that they could be setting themselves up to be an earthbound spirit, as could people who have so made another person such the centerpiece of their existence that their loss would permanently cripple them emotionally. That's not to say that grief itself could result in a person becoming a ghost, but the inability to come to terms with it that could do the trick.

The Mission Ghost:

A generally more 'upbeat' and even lively entity, his type of ghost stays around in order to take care of some unfinished business that was cut short by their unexpected death. This 'mission' can be as simple as revealing the location of a hidden will or as major as trying to find justice for a life cut short by murder, but in either case 'mission ghosts' seem intent upon achieving some goal they've set before themselves and feel they cannot rest until they have been succeeded. As such, they will often be among the most persistent and frequently appearing type of manifestation, for they have important things to do. On the flip side, they are generally also a short term entity, interacting within the physical realm only long enough to accomplish their goal, after which they abruptly move on. As such, 'mission ghosts' are usually gone in a few weeks or within a couple of months at most.

A unique type of 'mission ghost' is the 'legacy ghost.' This is a personality that stays not to accomplish some specific task, but to continue to interact with the physical realm as an outlet for its creativity. The case of Mrs. Rosemary Brown of England is a classic example of this sort of manifestation. In 1964 this widow and untutored musician who possessed only the most basic knowledge of the piano began composing sophisticated works that she claimed were dictated to her by the spirits of Liszt, Chopin, and Beethoven (among others.) Over a period of almost ten years she wrote a number of unique and never before heard symphonies of tremendous complexity and professionalism in the styles of several famous musicians, pieces which were largely beyond her own ability to play and that were identified by several professional musicians as consistent with the styles of these great composers. Though there were critics who also contended the pieces to be something 'less than' these composers best stuff, the fact that an amateur piano player could consistently produce anything even similar to the works of the great masters is nothing short of remarkable, and may constitute excellent evidence that the personality not only survives death, but may be capable of returning centuries after its demise to continue on with its life work.

The Goodbye or Comfort Ghost:

Perhaps the most common rationale for a personality manifesting to the still living remains the desire to say farewell. As such, the 'goodbye ghost' is a manifestation that appears—often only once—to either say goodbye to a loved one bereaved by their loss or to simply send a signal that they are well and have passed over successfully.

These manifestations can be as simple as turning on lights or tuning a radio to a particular station the deceased was known to favor while alive to something as dramatic as a full-body manifestation. Tales of widows seeing their late husband sitting on the foot of their bed or children encountering the manifestation of their dead sibling in their bedroom are legion, and even recently departed family pets have even been occasionally reported. However, these reports must be examined within the context of the many ways grief can manifest itself in one's imagination to produce the very fantasy a bereaved loved one 'needs' to bring closure to a tragic event. Yet if all such occurrences are psychosomatically induced, they should be exceedingly common and, perhaps, even anticipated among grieving relatives, though that has not proven to be the case. Such instances are still relatively uncommon and, more often than not, entirely unexpected and sometimes even undesirable, thereby reducing the chances that such visitations are hysterically-induced hallucinations. Trauma and excessive grief may account for some cases, but certainly not for all of them.

The Curious Ghost: Ghosts that remain around for long periods of time and seem to be willing to appear to almost anyone could be caused by personalities who know full well that they are dead and are quite comfortable with the fact, but have found the ability to manifest so fascinating that they are choosing to purposely haunt a location-if not for fun-at least out of curiosity. Certainly the desire to experiment might be a powerful inducement to get a ghost to interact with the physical realm, their motive being not to say goodbye or settle some unfinished business, but simply to see what they can do. It's not inconceivable that they may even be learning to manifest the necessary energy required to appear to us, honing their manifestation skills the same way an earthbound musician might hone his piano playing skills.

I'd imagine that those personalities who in life demonstrated a considerable curiosity about the afterlife or were of a scientific mind might find the opportunity to manipulate matter and energy from the other side to be too good an opportunity to pass up. Perhaps there are even paranormal investigators working the equation from the other side and are even now hard at work trying to demonstrate the existence of the spiritual realm as determinedly as some 'ghost hunters' are trying to do from this side. After all, reports of deceased paranormal investigators trying to communicate with their previous colleagues and students are not unknown, making it perhaps only a matter of time before the spiritual and physical realms get together to produce irrefutable proof that human consciousness survives the death of the brain that houses it, and so forcing science to start from scratch in defining what constitutes reality.

I would suspect such personalities, however, to be fairly rare and frequently frustrated in their efforts to get through to us 'thick mortals', and so wonder if they might not be prone to tiring of the game and move on to explore other realms of the spirit. After all, if they are curious enough to attempt to manifest within linear time and space, we can assume they might just as easily grow curious enough about other aspects of the ethereal realm to abandon their 'haunting experiments' and move on.

(Continued On Page 65)

TARA GREENE

Metaphysician, Tarot Reader, Astrologer, Psychic

Tara Greene is a natural born psychic, she remembers that we are immortal souls and multi-dimensional human beings. Tara's entire life is a spiritual quest devoted to self-actualization to help assist to awaken others. Tara has experienced many amazing metaphysical events which have guided and shaped her life. Tara is a certified Transformational Psychotherapist, a professional spiritual psychic and life coach with over 23 years' experience with over 29,000 clients using Tarot, Astrology and Dreams as metaphysical tools. Tara leads corporate communications workshops, women's spirituality workshops, teaches courses and online workshops and leads healing ceremonies in Sedona Arizona. She has travelled to numerous sacred sites where she received transformational initiations. Tara has studied with numerous teachers, Tibetan Buddhist, Peruvian shamans, Psychotherapeutic workshops, Susun Weed, Starhawk, as well as her own spirit guides. Tara apprenticed with and trained in shamanic healing with Oriah Mountain Dreamer. Tara loves to write, sing, drum , and creates CD's of channeled meditations. Tara is the Official Tarot Card Reader and Astrologer of The 'X' Zone Radio/TV Show. Tara is available for worldwide readings through her website at www.taratarot.com.

www.TaraTarot.com

Understanding The Psychology Of Ghosts
Continued From Page 63

As such, while curious ghosts might prove the most likely type to help us demonstrate the existence of a spiritual realm, they may also be among the most 'flighty' in that the very curiosity that makes them willing to try and communicate with us makes them equally likely to leave to explore other aspects of their new existence as well, which would at least be consistent with their personality.

The Mischievous Ghost:

Similar to the curious ghost but of a somewhat more menacing vein is that which we call the mischievous or 'playful' ghost. It is different from the curious ghost in that it isn't as interested in demonstrating the reality of the supernatural realm as it is in simply frightening the still living. It is as though haunting is one great amusement to it, and it will spend any amount of energy necessary to play the game for as long as it can.

Obviously, then, such ghosts are immature and childish (like the personalities behind them) and are comparable to the practical joker who thinks everything he does is hilarious and can't understand why others can't see the humor in his often mean spirited and usually embarrassing shenanigans. It can also be among the most frightening type of ghost in that it is actually trying to scare people (whereas most ghosts do so unintentionally.) This can manifest itself in something as innocent as making a chair rock, hiding a piece of jewelry or pulling the sheets off a bed or to something as serious as tugging hair, slapping, or even tripping people! Clearly, they are, at a minimum, the most difficult sort to live with for they want to make a nuisance of themselves and, in fact, go out of their way to make living with them almost impossible.

Additionally, being that these are very interactive ghosts, they may be the source of at least some-if not all-poltergeist activity. This is not a popular theory, however, for poltergeists are frequently though to be the result not of a ghostly entity, but of uncontrolled bursts of psychic or telekinetic energy put out by a particular living person. However, as with most ghostly theories, it could just as well be that mischievous ghosts are able to utilize the traumatic energy such a person puts out as a means of moving things; in other words, a nervous teenage girl may simply be the perfect conduit for inadvertently providing the very energy a mischievous entity requires to do it's mischief, without which it would be unable to manifest itself. This would also explain why poltergeist activity frequently ceases when the 'source energy' (the person) leaves the vicinity-it no longer has a source of energy-or why it sometimes follows the individual to other places (the ghost is attracted to their energy and follows them.) Of course, this doesn't explain why all similarly high strung teenagers don't have poltergeist activity happening around them all the time (such activity is, after all, comparatively rare.) One possibility is that such ghosts are themselves exceedingly rare, or that

people put out different psychic energies and mischievous entities are attracted to only certain types (or, perhaps, frequencies?). In any case, the idea that there are personalities willing to pull stunts on the still living should be no more remarkable than the fact that such fortunately uncommon individuals exist in the physical realm today. An immature personality is no more likely to suddenly 'grow up' once it is dead than a mature one is likely to revert to it's second childhood once it dies. People will always be people, after all, regardless of whether they are dead or alive.

The Angry Ghost:

While a mischievous ghost might be, at its heart, relatively benign and even potentially amusing at times, an angry ghost is another matter. Negative energy is a powerful force so the idea that anger, rage and hatred might keep a personality earthbound has to be considered. Certainly people have been willing to endure tremendous hardship and great personal loss in the quest for revenge, so the thought that an angry personality might be willing to endure the personal hell of an earthly wandering in search of vengeance is not difficult to imagine. In fact, it would be entirely consistent with what we know of human nature.

How the manifestation of an angry entity would 'look' and 'feel' is a source for considerable debate. It could be as simple as an oppressive or uncomfortable feeling one might experience upon entering a particular room to something as frightening as an air of overpowering hatred and dread hanging in the atmosphere . In more extreme cases, it may even manifest poltergeist-like activity and do such things as hurl objects at the observer or even physically attack a person, so the ability of an angry ghost to do real damage should never be minimized or ignored.

In any case, the angry ghost has gotten itself so deeply enmeshed within the periphery of the physical realm that it is truly stuck and, in some cases, may be entirely incapable of moving on to higher plains of existence (without perhaps considerable help from other

spiritual entities.) Could this be one reason religion frequently teaches the importance of forgiveness and controlling ones anger? Fortunately such entities are relatively rare, but even so they present the greatest challenge to the ghost hunter, for they truly are capable of being dangerous, especially if one feeds into their anger by sending out the very same negative emotions they are sensing from them. Anger is a destructive force that grows more powerful with time and can only be dissipated through the power of love and compassion.

It should be obvious by now that there many reasons for becoming a ghost, most of them having to do with human nature and our base personalities. Everything from love and concern for those left behind to curiosity and immaturity to outright hatred for the living are all reasons anyone could become—at least briefly—a ghost. In that regards, then, becoming a ghost appears to be something that can be both voluntary and accidental, and in some cases may even be unconscious.

On the other hand, it also seems likely that most people will never become a ghost but will instead choose to move on to grandeur, more magnificent vistas immediately after they die. Of course, this doesn't mean they are no longer a part of our lives. After all, a ghost is the manifestation of a personality, and that personality—and the person it represents—can live on and even express itself without having to manifest itself in the physical realm at all, which not only demonstrates the power of the human consciousness, but the power of love as well. There is no more powerful force in the universe and, in fact, may be all that truly exists within the context of the absolute. []

LIQUID DIAMOND

IN THE WILDERNESS OF RUSSIA...

...ten-year-old Natalia falls through a cave portal known as the Liquid Diamond and lands in a world filled with mythical creatures. Here amongst cockatrices, blemmyes and elves, Natalia meets Catalyst, a boy of half-human, half-krusnik vampire hunter descent. The two – along with their huge and hairy Basajaunak herdsman friend – are thrown into a quest to find the crystals that keep the portal locked shut. Without the crystals in place, war will break out between the human world and the kingdoms in the other realm. Friends at her side, Natalia must face unknown evils or lose her own home for good.

Liquid Diamond is the first novel in Sebastien Blue's mythology and monster based series. Look out for his next book, Natalia's Return!

Liquid Diamond is available for order through Amazon, Chapters, and Barnes & Noble. The eBook edition is available for download for Kindle, Nook, Kobo, iTunes, and GooglePlay.

By Sebastien Blue

ABOUT SEBASTIEN BLUE...

Author Sebastien Blue has been a voracious reader of worldwide classical literature and a huge fan of horror movies since he was a boy. His love of foreign folklore and mythology inspired him launch his first book series. Blue is a strong believer that, in addition to providing entertainment, young adult books should provide empowering and encouraging messages. Rising from an impoverished background, and facing struggles with dyslexia, Sebastien Blue's ultimate goal is to promote literacy and creativity.

Blue is currently available to book media events. Please contact him directly through this website if you would like to book an interview or have him attend an event.

Sebastien Blue presently resides in Peterborough, Ontario and looks forward to his next published works Natalia's Works.

www.SebastienBlue.com

Conspiracy Theories

The JFK Assassination
This much we can stipulate: President John F. Kennedy was assassinated on Nov. 22, 1963, struck by two bullets — one in the head, one in the neck — while riding in an open-topped limo through Dealey Plaza in Dallas. Lee Harvey Oswald was charged with killing him, and a presidential commission headed by Chief Justice Earl Warren found that Oswald acted alone.

That conclusion hasn't passed muster with the public. A 2003 ABC News poll found that 70% of Americans believe Kennedy's death was the result of a broader plot. The trajectory of the bullets, some say, didn't square with Oswald's perch on the sixth floor of the Texas School Book Depository. Others suggest a second gunman — perhaps on the grassy knoll of Dealey Plaza — participated in the shooting. Others believe in an even broader conspiracy. Was Kennedy killed by CIA agents acting either out of anger over the Bay of Pigs or at the behest of Vice President Lyndon Johnson? By KGB operatives? Mobsters mad at Kennedy's brother for initiating the prosecution of organized crime rings? Speculation over one of history's most famous political assassinations is such a popular parlor game that most people have taken the rumors to heart: just 32% of those polled by ABC believe Oswald carried out the killing on his own.

9/11 Cover-Up
Not since the JFK assassination has there been a national tragedy so heavily imprinted in American minds — or that has given rise to quite as many alternative explanations. While videos and photographs of the two planes striking the World Trade Center towers are famous around the world, the sheer profusion of documentary evidence has only provided even more fodder for conspiracy theories.

A May 2006 Zogby poll found that 42% of Americans believed that the government and the 9/11 commission "concealed or refused to investigate critical evidence that contradicts their official explanation of the September 11th attacks." Why had the military failed to intercept the hijacked planes? Had the government issued a "stand down" order, to minimize interference with a secret plan to destroy the buildings and blame it on Islamic terrorists? In 2005, Popular Mechanics published a massive investigation of similar claims and responses to them. The reporting team found that the North American Aerospace Defense Command (NORAD) did not have a history of having fighter jets prepped and ready to intercept aircraft that had gone off route. And while the team found no evidence that the government had planned the attacks, lack of proof has rarely stopped conspiracy theorists before.

Area 51 and the Aliens
We may have Tang thanks to the space program, but who gave us such innovations as the Stealth fighter and Kevlar? Aliens, of course. Conspiracy theorists believe that the remains of crashed UFO spacecrafts are stored at Area 51, an Air Force base about 150 miles from Las Vegas, where government scientists reverse-engineer the aliens' highly advanced technology. Fodder for this has come from a variety of supposed UFO sightings in the area and testimony from a retired Army colonel who says he was given access to extraterrestrial materials gathered from an alien spacecraft that crashed in Roswell, N.M. Some believe that the government studies time travel at Area 51, also known as Groom Lake or Dreamland.

Secret Societies Control the World
If you were really a member of the global élite, you'd know this already: the world is ruled by a powerful, secretive few. Many of the rest of us peons have heard that in 2004 both candidates for the White House were members of Yale University's secretive Skull and Bones society, many of whose members have risen to powerful positions. But Skull and Bones is small potatoes compared with the mysterious cabals that occupy virtually every seat of power, from the corridors of government to the boardrooms of Wall Street.

Take the Illuminati, a sect said to have originated in 18th century Germany and which is allegedly responsible for the pyramid-and-eye symbol adorning the $1 bill: they intend to foment world wars to strengthen the argument for the creation of a worldwide government (which would, of course, be Satanic in nature). Or consider the Freemasons, who tout their group as the "oldest and largest worldwide fraternity" and boast alumni like George Washington. Some think that despite donating heaps of cash to charity, they're secretly plotting your undoing at Masonic temples across the world. Or maybe, some theorize, the guys pulling the strings aren't concealed in shadow at all. They might be the intelligentsia on the Council on Foreign Relations, a cadre of policy wonks who allegedly count their aims as publishing an erudite bimonthly journal and establishing a unified world government — not necessarily in that order.

The Moon Landings Were Faked
It's now been nearly four decades since Neil Armstrong took his "giant leap for mankind" — if, that is, he ever set foot off this planet. Doubters say the U.S. government, desperate to beat the Russians in the space race, faked the lunar landings, with Armstrong and Buzz Aldrin acting out their mission on a secret film set, located (depending on the theory) either high in the Hollywood Hills or deep within Area 51. With the photos and videos of the Apollo missions only available through NASA, there's no independent verification that the lunar landings were anything but a hoax.

The smoking gun? Film of Aldrin planting a waving American flag on the moon, which critics say proves that he was not in space. The flag's movement, they say, clearly shows the presence of wind, which is impossible in a vacuum. NASA says Aldrin was twisting the flagpole to get the moon soil, which caused the flag to move. (And never mind that astronauts have brought back hundreds of independently verified moon rocks.) Theorists have even suggested that filmmaker Stanley Kubrick may have helped NASA fake the first lunar landing, given that his 1968 film 2001: A Space Odessey proves that the technology existed back then to artificially create a spacelike set. And as for Virgil I. Grissom, Edward H. White and Roger B. Chaffee — three astronauts who died in a fire while testing equipment for the first moon mission? They were executed by the U.S. government, which feared they were about to disclose the truth.

Far-fetched as the hoax theory may seem, a 1999 Gallup poll showed that it's comparatively durable: 6% of Americans said they thought the lunar landings were fake, and 5% said they were undecided.

Jesus and Mary Magdalene
Jesus and Mary Magdalene might have been married, or so says the Gospel of Philip. Sure, it's the basic plot of The Da Vinci Code (the thriller also wraps in conspiracy shibboleths like Opus Dei and the Knights Templar for good measure) — but the theory finds its basis in writings from the Gnostic Gospels, which were discovered in 1945 and whose authenticity religious experts still dispute. In the Gospel of Philip, Mary Magdalene, who is referred to as Jesus' koinonos, a Greek term for "companion" or "partner," is depicted as being closer to Jesus than any other apostle.

In an exchange between Peter and Mary, he admits to her that "the Saviour loved you above all other women" — a tense moment in the scripture that seems to portray the jealousy that the other apostles might have felt for Mary's relationship with Jesus. The only other evidence used to support the theory is a mention of Jesus kissing Mary often, but some say kissing was the custom and it was typical of Jesus to practice it with those close to him. (Remember Judas?)

Holocaust Revisionism
Despite overwhelming evidence and an admission and apology from Germany decades ago, revisionists continue to claim that nearly 6 million Jews were not killed by Nazis during the Holocaust. Iranian President Mahmoud Ahmadinejad, for one, has called the Holocaust a "myth" and suggested that Germany and other European countries, rather than Palestine, provide land for a Jewish state.

Unlike Ahmadinejad, most revisionists do not deny that Jews were interned in prison camps during World War II; rather, they argue that the number of deaths was greatly exaggerated. Gas chambers are a particular sticking point: Holocaust deniers say they were purely a rumor or, if they indeed existed, were not powerful enough to kill — though evidence and history indicate otherwise. And the photographs of emaciated and dying Jews? Attorney Edgar J. Steele, a revisionist, says, "All those pictures of skinny people and bodies stacked like cordwood were actually of Czechs and Poles and Germans [who] died of typhus, which was rampant in the camps."[]

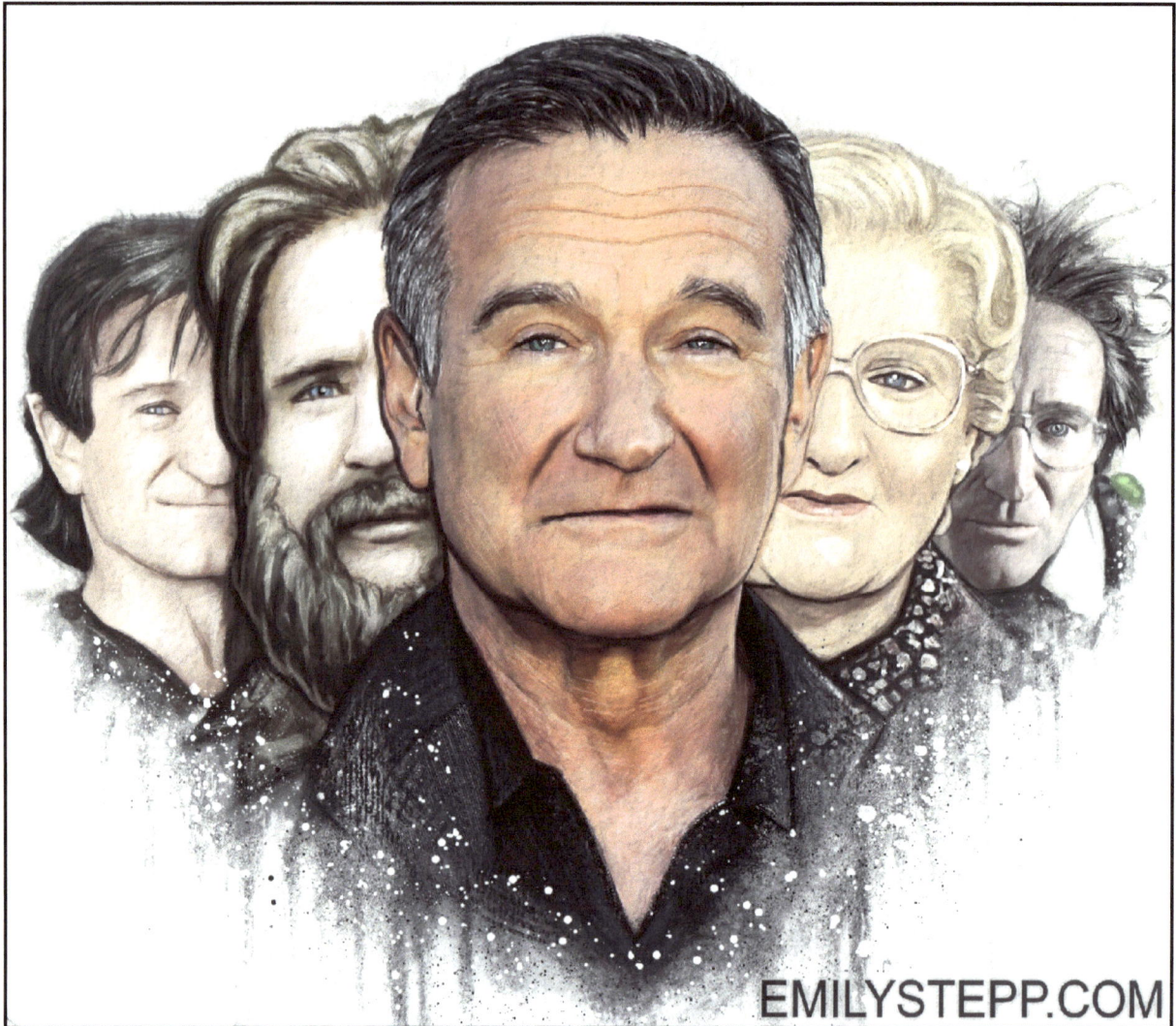

EMILYSTEPP.COM

The Passing Of
ROBIN WILLIAMS
1951 - 2014

When the notion of getting in touch with one's inner child entered popular currency, the standup comedian and actor Robin Williams, who has died aged 63 in a suspected suicide, was ripe to be its poster-boy. Partly it was his limitless energy and floodlight smile, or the frantic chatter that made it sound as if he were constantly interrupting himself or speaking in tongues. But he also resembled strongly a hirsute toddler who had broken out of the playpen to make whoopee.

Many of his most popular performances were as child-men rampaging through the prissy adult world. His breakthrough came as the naïve extra-terrestrial Mork in the US sitcom Mork & Mindy, which ran from 1978 to 1982. For that part, the red-and-silver costume that he donned for a monologue at the end of each episode even resembled an infant's romper suit. In Good Morning, Vietnam (1987), he played the real-life DJ Adrian Cronauer, whose wackiness in the face of war made him a hit with American troops. A swerve into straighter acting, as the literature teacher who challenges convention at a stuffy school in the late-1950s in Dead Poets

Society (1989), did not upset this trend. Instead, he transferred deftly his comic skills into a dramatic setting as his character liberated pupils formerly rigid with obedience.

Williams did not need to be visible on screen to continue his campaign of disinhibition: some of his most pure and untamed work was as the voice of the Genie in Disney's Aladdin (1992), for which he improvised the lion's share of his dialogue while the animators worked around his ad-libs. Any magic that film exudes is largely down to him. It was with a certain inevitability that Williams was cast as the boy who was supposed never to grow up, but did, in Steven Spielberg's Peter Pan sequel Hook (1992), and as a child with an ageing disorder that made him appear to be an adult in Francis Ford Coppola's Jack (1996).

Had these movies been better, or more beloved, they might have been known as Williams's signature roles. That status should go instead to his deranged, emotionally naked (and sometimes physically naked) performance in Terry Gilliam's The Fisher King (1991) as a homeless man whose search for the Holy Grail is born out of trauma. He was Oscar-nominated for that, as well as for Good Morning, Vietnam and Dead Poets Society; he finally won for playing a bereaved therapist in Good Will Hunting (1997).

But no performer who had been through

the extreme addictions and depression that Williams had (and about which he was candid in his standup routines and interviews) could fail to be aware of his own capacity for darkness. It was this that he gradually began to draw on in a run of serious and even abrasive parts which made the latter stages of his career arguably the most interesting (if the least amusing). Chief among these was Christopher Nolan's Insomnia (2002), in which he played a suspected murderer hunted by a cop (played by Al Pacino). In the same year, he also starred as a children's entertainer driven to madness when he is usurped by a younger rival in the bitter comedy Death to Smoochy, and as a lonely photo-counter employee who develops an unhealthy obsession with a family in the thriller One Hour Photo. Though he had not forsaken lighter material altogether, the impression was unmistakable that of a clown wiping off his makeup to show the tears underneath.

Williams was born in Chicago, Illinois, to Laura, a fashion model, and Robert, a senior executive at Ford Motor Company. He endured a lonely childhood in which he played mostly on his own in the large family home and was bullied at school for being overweight. The family moved to Marin County, California, when Williams was 16.

(Continued On Page 69)

The Passing Of
ROBIN WILLIAMS
1951 - 2014
Continued From Page 68

He was then educated at Claremont Men's College, where he studied political science and also took improvisation acting classes. He went on to study acting, first at the College of Marin and later at the Juilliard School, New York, from which he graduated in 1976. He auditioned for acting jobs but was forced to earn money instead working as a bartender and in an ice-cream parlour.

After he began working the standup circuit in Los Angeles, he got early breaks on TV shows including The Richard Pryor Show and in a small part in the sex comedy Can I Do It 'Til I Need Glasses (1977). His zany audition for the small role of Mork in two episodes of the long-running sitcom Happy Days led the producer Garry Marshall to remark that Williams was the only alien to try out for the part: "I will never forget the day I met him and he stood on his head in my office chair and pretended to drink a glass of water using his finger like a straw."

His instant popularity guaranteed a spin-off series in which he muddled through earthly life with the help of a sympathetic housemate played by Pam Dawber. "The first season of Mork & Mindy I knew immediately that a three-camera format would not be enough to capture Robin and his genius talent," said Marshall. "So I hired a fourth camera operator and he just followed Robin. Only Robin. Looking back, four cameras weren't enough. I should have hired a fifth camera to follow him too." The show was a ratings hit, and Mork's nonsensical utterings, including his greeting "Nanu-nanu", became unlikely catchphrases. It was here that the child-like persona on which Williams's career was founded began to take shape.

The actor's first major film role was as the lead in Robert Altman's live-action version of Popeye (1980). Despite being financed by Disney, this oddball musical was very much an Altman movie, throwing caution and sometimes coherence to the wind. But Williams, bearing engorged prosthetic forearms and sounding unintelligible at times with a pipe lodged in the corner of his mouth, was both perfect and hypnotically strange in the part, opposite Shelley Duvall as Olive Oyl. In later films, he would be the eyecatching main attraction, ceding the spotlight to no one. Here, he was just one among many outlandish elements.

In the pictures that immediately followed, he was positively restrained, as though not yet confident that his Morkishness could work in movies. He was the unassuming hero of an adaptation of John Irving's novel The World According to Garp (1982) and the least wacky participant in the desert-island comedy Club Paradise (1986). But he showed, as a newly fired executive who averts a robbery in The Survivors (1983) and as a Russian saxophonist defecting to the US in Moscow on the Hudson (1984), that his unpredictable but essentially comforting persona was flexible enough to work in a variety of settings. His first hit movie, Good Morning, Vietnam, followed

soon after, cementing for cinemagoers an image of Williams to rival the one TV audiences had enjoyed in Mork. The film could be mawkish, as could Williams himself, but this was tempered by its authentic irreverence.

The same could not be said of all Williams's later films. There had always been a needy aspect to even his most scabrous standup routines, and he was never a dangerous comic: inflammatory material was rendered essentially fireproof by those love-me eyes, that gurning grin. Cinema, with its aggrandising close-ups and urging, saccharine scores, could sometimes be his worst enemy. Dead Poets Society had its share of sappiness, not least in the climax in which the students climb onto their desks and salute Williams with Walt Whitman's line "O Captain! My Captain!" The star, to his credit, underplayed admirably.

This was not the case in those films that earned him a reputation as a sentimentalist. He twinkled unstoppably throughout Awakenings (1990), in which he played Dr Malcolm Sayer, based loosely on Dr Oliver Sacks, and in Toys (1992), where he was the pure-hearted saviour of a toy factory. Mrs Doubtfire (1993) provided an opportunity for Williams to let rip anarchically as a father bonding with his estranged children by posing as their Scottish nanny. That also gave him another smash-hit. But he was pimping for tears and goosebumps again as a man exploring the afterlife in What Dreams May Come, as a doctor trying to prove that laughter is the best medicine in Patch Adams (both 1998), as a simpering android in Bicentennial Man and as a Jewish shopkeeper fostering hope in the ghettoes of Nazi-occupied Poland in Jakob the Liar (both 1999).

Williams had also been forging a separate career as a pillar of family entertainment in adventures such as Jumanji (1995) and Flubber (1997). This continued when he played Teddy Roosevelt in two Night at the Museum films (2006 and 2009); a third, in which he also appears, is due for release later this year.

His decision to branch out into more challenging material in the early 2000s came directly after a stretch of ingratiating parts. But unlike, say, Bill Murray's transformation into an

indie icon after Lost in Translation, Williams's work in films such as Insomnia felt for all its sincerity like a graft that did not take. His image as a human teddy-bear persisted even after he made World's Greatest Dad (2009), a film he admired greatly, in which he played a father who fabricates his son's diaries after the boy dies in an auto-erotic accident. Williams's attempts to kill off his cutesy persona were very much of the one-step-forward, two-steps-back variety. For every World's Greatest Dad or One Hour Photo, there were many more like the lacklustre comedies RV: Runaway Vacation (2006) or Old Dogs (2009). He was, however, a surprising addition to the cast of The Butler (2013), in which he played Eisenhower.

Williams's work-rate in the last decade was arrested by health problems and by occasional relapses into addiction, the most recent of which incurred a spell in rehab. He had returned to standup in 2008 with a show entitled Weapons of Self-Destruction, though this was interrupted briefly by surgery to replace an aortic valve. "You appreciate little things," he said after that procedure, "like walks on the beach with a defibrillator."

He is survived by his third wife, Susan Schneider, whom he married in 2011; his son Zachary, from his first marriage, to Valerie Velardi, which ended in divorce; and by his daughter, Zelda, and son, Cody, from his second marriage, to Marsha Garces, which ended in divorce. []

BOBCHA'S CORNER

by Bobcha

I DIDN'T KNOW THAT

* Glass takes one million years to decompose, which means it never wears out and can be recycled an infinite amount of times!
* Gold is the only metal that doesn't rust, even if it's buried in the ground for thousands of years.
* Your tongue is the only muscle in your body that is attached at only one end.
* If you stop getting thirsty, you need to drink more water. When a human body is dehydrated, its thirst mechanism shuts off.
* Zero is the only number that cannot be represented by Roman numerals.
* Kites were used in the American Civil War to deliver letters and newspapers.
* The song, Auld Lang Syne, is sung at the stroke of midnight in almost every English-speaking country in the world to bring in the new year.
* Drinking water after eating reduces the acid in your mouth by 61 percent.
* Peanut oil is used for cooking in submarines because it doesn't smoke unless it's heated above 450F.
* The roar that we hear when we place a seashell next to our ear is not the ocean, but rather the sound of blood surging through the veins in the ear.
* Nine out of every 10 living things live in the ocean.
* The banana cannot reproduce itself. It can be propagated only by the hand of man.
* Airports at higher altitudes require a longer airstrip due to lower air density.
* The University of Alaska spans four time zones.
* The tooth is the only part of the human body that cannot heal itself.
* In ancient Greece , tossing an apple to a girl was a traditional proposal of marriage. Catching it meant she accepted.
* Warner Communications paid $28 million for the copyright to the song Happy Birthday.
* Intelligent people have more zinc and copper in their hair.
* A comet's tail always points away from the sun.
* The Swine Flu vaccine in 1976 caused more death and illness than the disease it was intended to prevent.
* Caffeine increases the power of aspirin and other painkillers, that is why it is found in some medicines.
* The military salute is a motion that evolved from medieval times, when knights in armor raised their visors to reveal their identity.
* If you get into the bottom of a well or a tall chimney and look up, you can see stars, even in the middle of the day.
* When a person dies, hearing is the last sense to go. The first sense lost is sight.
* In ancient times strangers shook hands to show that they were unarmed.
* Strawberries are the only fruits whose seeds grow on the outside.
* Avocados have the highest calories of any fruit at 167 calories per hundred grams.
* The moon moves about two inches away from the Earth each year.
* The Earth gets 100 tons heavier every day due to falling space dust.
* Due to earth's gravity it is impossible for mountains to be higher than 15,000 meters.
* Mickey Mouse is known as "Topolino" in Italy .
* Soldiers do not march in step when going across bridges because they could set up a vibration which could be sufficient to knock the bridge down.
* Everything weighs one percent less at the equator.
* For every extra kilogram carried on a space flight, 530 kg of excess fuel are needed at lift-off.
* The letter J does not appear anywhere on the periodic table of the elements.

BOBCHA'S CLEVER KITCHEN HINTS

* The simplest way to slice a bunch of cherry tomatoes is to sandwich them between two plastic lids and run a long knife through all of them at once!
* Keep brown sugar soft by storing with a couple of marshmallows.
* Deodorize sponges in the microwave. Soak in water spiked with white vinegar or lemon juice and put on fill power for one minute. Use tongs to remove as it will be hot!
* Boil orange peel and cloves to get rid of unpleasant smells in the kitchen.
* Hang onions in cut-up tights or old stockings to make them last for months!
* Create a thrifty watering can by puncturing holes in the top of a used milk bottle.
* Store cupcake and muffin cases in a mason jar.
*Remove pet hair from furniture and carpets with a rubber squeegee.
* Cover paint trays with aluminum foil to make cleaning up afterwards a breeze.
* Place a layer of waxed paper on top of kitchen cupboards to prevent grease and dust from settling. Switch out every few months to keep them clean.
* Easily draw out a splinter for easy removal by applying a paste of baking soda and water.
* Water straight from the tap becomes cloudy when frozen. To make ice cubes crystal clear, allow a kettle of boiled water to cool slightly and use this to fill your ice cube trays.
* To prevent potatoes budding, add an apple in the bag.
* Add half a teaspoon of baking soda to the water when hard-boiling eggs to make the shells incredibly easy to peel off.
* Tie a sprig of eucalyptus to your shower head. The steam will help infuse your bathroom with an invigorating fragrance.
* Use non-stick cooking spray in votive holders to prevent wax from sticking to the sides.
* WD 40 can be used to remove crayon marks from any surface!
* To get rid of the musty smell on old towels, wash using 1 cup of white vinegar on a hot cycle, then repeat with 1/2 cup of bicarbonate of soda.
* Use a fork to press garlic when there isn't a garlic crusher available.
* When hanging a picture frame, put a dab of toothpaste on the frame where you need the nails to be. Then simply press against the wall to leave marks (which can later be wiped) as guides for hammering in.
* Put a dry towel in with a wet load to reduce the drying time (this really works, I've been doing it for years!)
* To tell if eggs are fresh, immerse them in a bowl of water. Fresh eggs will lie on the bottom, while stale eggs will float to the surface.
* Sprinkle salt in the spaces between patio slabs and at the bottom of walls to get rid of pesky weeds(but be careful NOT to get salt near plants you want to keep as salt will kill them!)
* Clean patio stones with a solution of 1/2 white vinegar and 1/2 water in a spray bottle. Leave for 10 minutes and rinse off (soiled areas may require a little scrubbing). Also helps get rid of weeds too!
* To clean a wooden chopping board, sprinkle on a handful of Kosher salt and rub with half a lemon. Rinse with clean water and dry to ensure it is clean and germ-free.
* Use ice-cubes to lift out indentations made by furniture on your carpets.
* To easily peel potatoes, boil with the skins on them immerse in cold water for 5 seconds. Then twist the potatoes between your hands and the skin will peel right off!
* To decorate a chocolate beautifully, lay a piece of lace over the cake and sprinkle icing sugar over the top.
* To stop the annoying sound of a dripping tap, tie a piece of string around the faucet which is long enough to reach down to the sink.
* Use rubber bands to help open a jar easily: place one around the jar lid and another around the middle of the glass. The rubber provides friction to prevent your hands from slipping.
* To prevent your eyes watering while chopping onions, wipe the chopping board with white vinegar (which won't affect the taste of the onions)
* Use ketchup to remove the tarnish from copper pans. Slather the pan with ketchup and leave for 30 minutes for the acid to break down the tarnish, then rinse clean and buff with a soft cloth.
* Store bed sheets inside their pillowcases for easy storage and access.
* Place a few drops of essential oil on the cardboard tube of a toilet roll to make your bathroom smell wonderful.
* Drop a couple of denture cleaning tablets into the toilet bowl at night to clean off stubborn stains.
* Use cupcake cases to cover drinks glasses in the summer and prevent flies from dropping in.
[]

Can a protein originally derived from a jellyfish improve your memory? Scientists say, "Yes!"

Can a simple protein hold the key to improving your memory?

Researchers have discovered a protein that actually supports healthy brain function.*

For many years, researchers have known that the human brain loses cells throughout our lives, part of the natural process of aging. In fact, we lose about 85,000 brain cells per day, that is one per second, over 31 million brain cells every year! This impacts every aspect of your life...how you think and how you feel.

Recently, scientists made a significant breakthrough in brain health with the discovery that apoaequorin can support healthy brain function, help you have a sharper mind, and think clearer.*

Supports Healthy Brain Function*

Apoaequorin is in the same family of proteins as those found in humans, but it was originally discovered in one of nature's simplest organisms — the jellyfish.

Supports a Sharper Mind*

Now produced in a scientific process, researchers formulated this vital protein into a product called Prevagen®. Prevagen is clinically shown to help with mild memory problems associated with aging.*

Improves Memory*

This type of protein is vital and found naturally in the human brain and nervous system. As we age we can't make enough of them to keep up with the brain's demands. Prevagen supplements these proteins during the natural process of aging to keep your brain healthy. Prevagen comes in an easy-to-swallow capsule. It has no known side effects and will not interact with your current medication.

Supports Clearer Thinking*

Just how well does Prevagen work? In a computer assessed, double-blind, placebo-controlled study, Prevagen improved memory for most subjects within 90 days.*

Try Prevagen® for yourself and feel the difference.

Get a Third Bottle FREE when you Buy Two!

Call toll-free (888) 859-6463 today!

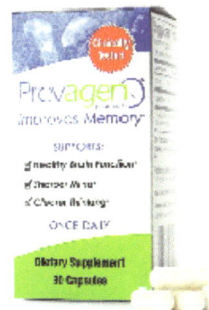

Future of God
A M E N

"Knowledge is a Wonderful Gift." - Ginex

Future of God
AMEN
A Call to Daughters and Sons of God

Nicholas P. Ginex

Providing a critical review of the Torah, New Testament, and Koran, author Nicholas P. Ginex's Future of God Amen explains the foundation of Egyptian beliefs—an integrated concept of truth, justice, righteousness, the soul, and a hereafter—and how these principles influenced the development of the Judaic, Christian, and Islamic religions.

It shares to today's worshippers information about the origin of God—that Jesus Christ acknowledged the Egyptian God Amen as "the beginning of the creation of God" (Revelation 3:14), which allows readers to gain a better understanding of their own personal God.

Moreover, the book also offers recommendations for religious leaders on working together in the spirit of unifying their scriptures as well as resolving their present differences.

An opportunity to widen one's spiritual scope, Future of God Amen is also an excellent resource for students of sociology, theology, psychology, and humanity studies.

"Mr Ginex deals masterfully with a great sweep of Egyptian history, closing the gap between our understanding and Egyptian understanding in most remarkable ways; for instance his explanation of ka or soul outstrips what many modern theologians can offer." Review by Mike Voyce

ABOUT THE AUTHOR: Nick Ginex is a retired Electrical Engineer with an MBA in Finance. He worked in design and distinguished himself in the support disciplines of Maintainability and Configuration Management (CM). As CM Manager of software and hardware products at top aerospace and commercial companies, his planning and organizational skills were applied for the successful operation of entire engineering projects. While writing this book, Ginex sang and played his guitar at senior care centers and nursing homes for their enjoyment. The smiles on their faces and joy in their eyes have been his greatest reward. His love for his children and desire to inform them about the God Amen and His influence on the Judaic, Christian, and Islamic religions - have motivated him to write this book. A book he hopes others will benefit by learning more about God and their purpose in life.

www.futureofgodamen.com

www.ingramcontent.com/pod-product-compliance
Lightning Source LLC
LaVergne TN
LVHW072106070426
835509LV00002B/31